NO BRYLCREEM - NO MEDALS

To Peter
With Best Wishes
Jack.

Published in 1999 by
WOODFIELD PUBLISHING, Bognor
Regis, West Sussex PO21 5EL, UK.

© Jack Hambleton, 1999

ISBN 0 873203 46 2

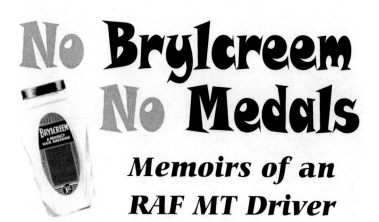

No Brylcreem No Medals

Memoirs of an RAF MT Driver

JACK HAMBLETON

Woodfield Publishing
BOGNOR REGIS • WEST SUSSEX • ENGLAND

To Dorothy, the beautiful girl I met,
fell in love with and married.

and to David Holmes, my son in law,
for his advice, assistance and patience.

NO BRYLCREEM - NO MEDALS

Contents

About the Author

Jack Hambleton is a writer of short nostalgic articles. His previous book, *Twentieth Century Ridgeway... remembered* was published in 1997.

Jack has a keen interest in people and their memories of times gone by. He has been interviewed on BBC Radio Sheffield and presents talks to local groups.

Acknowledgements

Cover photograph by permission of Brylcreem / Sara Lee Household Body Care.

Photograph of Clock Tower, Skegness, by permission of the *Grimsby Evening Telegraph*.

Photograph of Royal Air Force Catalina by permission of the David Legg Collection.

Photograph of Martin Baltimore Mark V by permission of *Flypast* magazine.

Nick Shepperd

Douglas Lamb

Vernon Crooks

Colin Moir

The Author's MT Section in Egypt, 1944

NO BRYLCREEM - NO MEDALS

Foreword

Sunday, the 3rd of September 1939, will always be remembered as the day the Second World War started. I was 15 years and 6 months of age, so the outbreak of a war to me was an event of great excitement filled with youthful visions of all the heroes it was to create. The first six months of the war did not have a great impact on me, but then came the Battle of Britain and I visualised myself as a famous fighter pilot, clearing the skies of enemy aircraft single-handed. By early 1942, realising the war was not progressing as well as it should be, I believed that come March when I would be 18 years of age, my presence in the armed forces would be sufficient to improve the British fortunes in the conflict. I enlisted in His Majesties Royal Air Force, gratefully accepting the shilling handed to me on his behalf.

Little did I realise on that warm, sunny day in June, when I received our monarch's 'bounty', that my experiences during the following four and a half years would include not only occasions of great humour and hilarity, which were numerous but also tragedies, of which there were too many.

How could I have guessed that while being stationed on the Shetland Islands, I would be taken prisoner by a British soldier, or that later I would be entertained by the crew of a Russian submarine in a night of vodka and beer drinking revelry only to be arrested the following morning for 'spying' when boarding the submarine looking for my friends of the previous evening! Or that on returning to the mainland, I would have the fortune (or misfortune, whichever way it can be envisaged) of transporting 20 Irish 'navvies' in Royal Air Force uniforms around the South of England and become involved in their high spirited antics and boisterous escapades, which would have driven a more fainthearted chap to desertion.

Neither would I have guessed that later, when stationed in that mysterious and romantic land of the Egyptian Pharaohs, I would aid and abet the camp bookie in the 'nobbling' of the favourite ass running in the Donkey Derby, and indulge in betting on the 'Cockroach Handicap' races on the steaming cookhouse walls, where the large fat beetles would fall into the corned beef stew; or that while driving the camp crash ambulance (blood wagon) I would be chased round the aerodrome perimeter by a Baltimore aircraft; or that other hair-raising moments would come when escaping an attempted Arab ambush or later, with two pals and armed with nothing but starting handles I would have to stand firm against a party of irate, unruly Arab workers.

Returning to England, I was to spend a short time in the most extraordinary and humorous military hospital the Army possessed. The 'goings on' by the so-called patients were had to be seen to be believed.

Those light-hearted moments were to be intermingled with unforgettable tragedies. In the early days in Skegness, during a German bomber raid on the town, I saw a party of airmen mown down by gunfire. On the Shetland Islands, I assisted in carrying of the dead and wounded from Norwegian Motor torpedo boats returning from action in German occupied Norwegian waters. In a dense West Sussex forest, I was first on the scene of a crashed Spitfire and wrapped the two halves of a young pilot's body in his parachute. Later, in the Middle East, I attended three plane crashes in a 36-hour period which claimed the lives of 12 airmen.

My own life was saved by only 30 seconds, when a colleague took my place in a wagon to drive an officer to a bombing range. Tragically, both men walked onto an unexploded bomb and were blown to bits.

Finally, when a typhoid epidemic swept through the camp, I was to spend five months in a military hospital. Of the 120 men who had contracted the disease, 24 were to die, among them five of my closest friends in the same ward as myself.

When I enlisted in the Royal Air Force, it was with the knowledge that members of that service were identified by the other armed forces as the BRYLCREEM BOYS. It was with great gratification to me to believe I would be able to obtain regular supplies of my favourite haircream. My optimism could not have been more distant from reality. In my four and a half years service of travelling from country to country and from camp to camp, I was to experience many humorous, but unsuccessful efforts to acquire a jar of the precious unobtainable commodity – BRYLCREEM! Hence the song we used to sing:

My Brylcreem lies over the ocean,
My Brylcreem lies over the sea,
My Brylcreem lies over the ocean,
Oh, bring back my brylcreem to me.

With apologies to the traditional song 'My Bonnie'

The Author – Jack 'Hamby' Hambleton, 1942.

NO BRYLCREEM - NO MEDALS

CHAPTER ONE

"H'AIRMAN, WHAT H'IS YER NUMBER"

On Wednesday, the 10th July 1942, I left Sheffield grasping a small brown attaché case. On arrival at Bedford railway station and looking for a luxury conveyance to transport me to RAF Cardington, I found myself climbing over the tail-board of a 3-ton Bedford lorry, still hanging on to my attaché case, then scrambling for a seat on a wooden form which collapsed, with twenty pairs of arms and legs all entangled together. We arrived at Cardington just as the bods had sorted themselves out.

Tumbling out of the wagon, we were directed straight into the clothing stores to be fitted out with our uniforms and supplied with kit bags. This proved to be a unique experience and a comedy of errors. Standing in a disorderly, noisy queue, I eventually arrived at a counter and was sternly scrutinised by a sergeant who, by an expert glance, could relate to his assistants the sizes of clothing I required.

After receiving these items and attempting to fit them on, I was left pondering on what the sergeant's vocation in 'Civvy Street' may have been, possibly an undertaker, in which case there must have been many problems fitting bodies into coffins made to his measurements.

The following morning came an appearance before an officer on the Selection Board, deciding which trade I was to be trained for. That did not take very long.

"What do you want to be?"

"A motor mechanic."

"Can you drive?"

"No."

"Well, train as an MT driver, then re-muster to a mechanic."

"Next please!"

My future determined in two minutes! I was destined to become a 'scruffy' – as MT drivers were affectionately known. During my service career I met men who were mechanics and unable to drive, having to learn later. I even had to teach some of them to drive!

We spent two days at Cardington where they must have thought we had the plague, being eager to get rid of us as quickly as possible. We were then on our way to breezy, bracing Skegness on the Lincolnshire coast for six weeks of square bashing, or as it turned out to be, promenade bashing! As a raw eighteen-year-old 'erk' I arrived at Skegness railway station on a dark, wet July evening in 1942, wearing a tunic two sizes too small, trousers two sizes too large and a greatcoat almost touching the ground.

The illuminations and amusements of Skegness's pre-war, carefree days had been stored away, the streets were in darkness, the houses blacked out and the beach a no-go area, separated from the promenade by rolls of barbed wire. The town of Skegness and its people, having previously been hosts to throngs of holidaymakers, were now being invaded by thousands of lads in Air Force blue. Nevertheless, they welcomed us.

The six weeks training were spent billeted in the Warwick, which, as with the other of the town's pre-war hotels situated on the promenade, had been commandeered by the RAF. These ex-hotels were used only for sleeping in. The rooms, having during pre-war years held one bed, were now so crammed with iron camp beds, so that if your bed was close to a wall, to get to the door you had to stride over the other lads, making sure you kicked the ones still asleep. The laughter and the gaiety of those long-ago, happy days may echo to this day through those rooms in the still of the night, but during the daytime, the shouting of the lads would be drowned by the curses of the sergeants and the corporals, who would have you believe, "You, my darlin's, may have broken your mothers hearts but you're not going to break mine!"

Corporal Barnes was an ancient character the Royal Army Flying Corps had forgotten to demob at the end of the First

Raw recruits at Skegness, 1942.

World War in 1918. 'Barnsey' would put his 'haitches' where they should not be and leave them out where they should be. At five foot six inches tall he would look up at you and bawl out, "H'airman, what h'is yer number." As you looked down into his wizened face and told him, he would reply, "When h'I joined, we 'ad no number, we knew h'everyone by their name!" The moment he walked away, he had forgotten you existed until the next day when the same old question was asked and the same old answer was repeated.

One of the RAF's favourite exercises, but not ours, was route marching. We soon discovered the surface of the Skegness roads and those of the surrounding country lanes to be hard. Returning from ten-mile slogs with feet blistered, raw and bloody, the only way we could get our stockings off was to soak them in bowls of hot water. On one of these excursions as we staggered down a lane, a dear old lady stood at her cottage garden gate with a bucketful of apples, handing them out one at a time and blessing us as we passed. It was the only way she could get rid of her apples!

Amongst my new mates or comrades, there were all types, shapes and sizes with the odd character thrown in. One I recall vividly was Ray Greensleeves, a Gypsy, who had been recruited from a fairground. Ray could neither read nor write, having obviously got his King's shilling by signing an X. We would vainly attempt to read out to him the letters he received from his family, but their writing was so indecipherable that we doubted our own reading ability. We decided to teach Ray to read and write. At the end of our six weeks training and after devoting many hours of our spare time to him (and he still could not read or write), the RAF did not think him suitable to help win the war. Ray was discharged, returning to the

Skegness, 1942.

JACK HAMBLETON

· 17

fairground to serve his king and country by dishing out wooden balls for people to try to knock over coconuts.

At the far end of the promenade the large pre-war amusement hall had been converted into the other ranks dining hall, different groups of personnel going for their meals at varied times, those times being changed from week to week. One morning, with Skegness covered by low cloud and a heavy rain falling, we were assembled outside the Warwick waiting to march to the dining hall for breakfast. A squad of about fifty airmen could be seen returning from the dining hall having had their meal. A plane was heard flying above the low clouds. It suddenly descended out of the sky, over the sea and then came in low over the Sun Castle. The marching airmen spotted it, running down Castleton Boulevard to take cover. The plane was a Junkers JU88 German Bomber.

As the front gunner opened fire, spraying Castleton Boulevard with bullets, we raced back into the billet just as the plane released a bomb, it's blast smashing windows in the room we had run into for cover, sending us scampering back into the road faster than we had left it. Realising the lads who had gone into Castleton Boulevard could be in difficulties, we rushed to see if we could be of any assistance. The scene resembled a battlefield. Some, in trying to take cover in the shrubbery in the centre of the road had been caught and mown down by the gunfire, a number of airmen had been killed and many wounded. The previous week and the week following this incident, our squad went to and returned from the dining hall for breakfast at the same times as that unfortunate squad.

Believing that the defences of Skegness should be strengthened – I never actually saw what those defences were, apart from rolls of entangled barbed wire along the beach –

the powers that be decided a Lewis gun should be installed on the end of the pier. The gun, like Barnsey, was a relic of the First World War. We got the job. Four lads were down below on the sands filling sandbags, while a mate and I were on the pier hoisting them up. We would have been better employed building sandcastles, I didn't think that damn gun would have fired anyway.

Between the promenade and the beach were what, in pre-war times, had been ornamental gardens with a stream running through them. This section was now being used as an assault course. We had been in Skegness on the training course only seven days when a high-ranking officer visited the area, requesting that he view 'the men' tackle the assault course. The commanding officer, wishing to impress his superior, sent us rookies. Not yet having been over the course, this task should obviously have been carried out by a squad of men just finishing their training.

Forty men took part. On one section of the assault course, we had to swing on an iron bar across a water channel. On reaching the middle, one of the lads froze with fright, those following on behind him became stuck, unable to move forward or go back. With aching arms and wrists, we dropped one by one into the water. That morning's exercise turned into a fiasco, finishing with a casualty list of over thirty injured and a steady stream of patients heading for Skegness Hospital. It was at first feared that I had sustained a broken jaw, as well as a good soaking. When X-rayed however, my jaw was found to be only badly bruised, but several of the lads had to remain in hospital. The commanding officer was courageous enough to realise his error, but what the 'big chief' thought of our performance we never found out. He probably retired in disgust or surrendered to the enemy!

This fiasco was followed by an another chaotic exercise on the sand dunes near Winthorpe, only to be informed by a yelling Barnsey from his position of safety on the road, "You silly bloody shower are in the middle of a land-mined area." The sight of twenty men tiptoeing, not through tulips, but among land-mines must have appeared funny to onlookers taking their dogs for a walk. We were far from amused!

That majestic building the Seacroft Hotel billeted the officers. Its long front lawns were used as a firing range where, fortunately, the targets were placed at the bottom end and not facing the hotel entrance. With our far from accurate shooting, the RAF would have been short of officers, most of our bullets missing the target and landing in the North Sea.

Another of our exercises to get fighting fit was scrubbing the floors of the Warwick. Barnsey would tread over the still wet floors to judge how big his footprints were and for a little man they were large.

There was little to do during our spare time in wartime Skegness. After the route marches and running up and down the promenade, we were too tired at the end of each day. We either played draughts, dominoes or decoded Ray the gypsy's letters from home. On two shillings pay a day, we could only afford one night out each week and that was Saturday. This was the night Skegness livened up, when the Royal Naval ratings from HMS Royal Arthur came to town. Having, before the war, been Butlins Holiday Camp, it was now a shore based Royal Naval Station. Lord Haw-Haw, the German broadcasting propagandist, believing HMS Royal Arthur to be a warship, was repeatedly claiming on the wireless that the Germans had sunk it!

With a limited supply of girls in the town, the night usually ended with a fight. This was unfortunate because, as I was to discover later in my travels, both in this country and overseas, the Royal Navy had a great respect for the Royal Air Force and vice versa.

My last recollection of wartime Skeggy was the night before I left, when the German Luftwaffe made another visit. With blazing guns and exploding bombs they left the Clock Tower surrounded by smoke and flames, but the clock, like the town, survived.

CHAPTER TWO

"OH CHRIST, NOT ANOTHER BLOODY ONE."

At the end of six long tiring weeks, having perfected that blasted assault course and having used up my supply of Civvy Street BRYLCREEM and being unable to buy any more, it was time to move on. Of the squad of forty men in the Warwick, ten of us had become close friends. We were now leaving Skegness to be trained for our selected trades, I was the only one taking an MT driving course, and so all alone, I travelled to Weeton, near Blackpool.

The first night on arriving at Weeton I strolled confidently into a noisy NAAFI canteen and politely asked for a jar of BRYLCREEM. A subdued hush came over the room as a hundred faces looked towards me, followed by roars of laughter. I had asked for the impossible! The counter assistant equally politely told me I could have a jar of Anzora. This was a concoction, falsely called hair cream, resembling Gloy paste, it was far more effective than any glue. Bloody Anzora was to plague me from NAAFI to NAAFI, country to country.

The driving course began. The first vehicle I drove was a 1938 Austin 8 saloon car owned by the British School of Motoring; the driving instructor, a retired Army Major. He never let up in claiming to have famous next door neighbours; Reginald Dixon (the organist) on one side of his house and

George Formby (the comedian) on the other side. Whether true or false, it pleased him to think we believed him. We would drive past what he claimed to be his home near Blackpool and it was certainly a big house. We then moved on to 15 cwt Bedfords followed by 3-ton Bedfords and finally to the big Thorneycroft wagons which, when you sat in the cab you imagined you were on the top of Blackpool Tower.

RAF Weeton was a massive camp. Although there were six large NAAFI's, we mainly used the Salvation Army canteen (they had no BRYLCREEM either). One evening, the NAAFI in the WAAF's section of the camp caught fire, being completely gutted. The Blackpool Fire Brigade arrived, extinguished the fire and were back at their station before the camp's fire tender crew had even got their appliance's engine started.

While the fire was raging and most men were trying to pinch anything they could lay their hands on, (what there was to pinch out of WAAF's canteen I could not imagine) two airmen sneaked into the WAAF's quarters and laid their hands on two of the girls. A parade was held the following morning to identify the culprits. The two WAAFs had to walk between innumerable lines, scrutinising about five hundred airmen. By the time they had finished, those two girls must have been pig sick of the sight of airmen. They had not recognised anyone, so it was all in vain, but not to the two lads who had taken advantage of the fire.

Another incident during the driving course occurred on a night driving exercise. In a pea-souper of a fog and driving 3-ton Bedfords, we were returning in convoy along the Preston to Blackpool road. The leader took the wrong turning and in true follow my leader tradition, we all finished up in the middle of St. Anne's. That was not the only time I got lost during my service career. The next time was in the Egyptian desert and more amusing.

Driving through Blackpool one morning and stopping at a set of traffic lights, another RAF training vehicle was waiting on the other side of the road, I saw and recognised a lad I had been to school with, Albert Marriott. There was only time to wave to each other. I was to meet Albert again two years later in rather different circumstances.

During the fifth week of the course, I caught influenza, going into the camp hospital for ten days. When I came out my pals had finished their course and moved on. I resumed from where I had left off, passing the examinations first time. I was then granted my first seven days leave, four months after leaving Sheffield. I never found the RAF generous at granting leaves, at least not to me.

Those seven days passed quickly. When I left Weeton, I had been issued with rail warrants and instructions to report after the leave to RAF Bunchrew in Aberdeenshire. Going into the Army Regimental Transport Office (RTO) on the Midland Railway Station in Sheffield, I enquired where this place was. I gave them their first problem of the day. The only Bunchrew they could locate was in Invernesshire and not Aberdeenshire.

After being waved off from the station platform by my current girl friend, her parents and my parents (the Lord Mayor of Sheffield was otherwise engaged and unable to attend such an historic occasion) I was on my way into the unknown, which in this case was true, with a long journey ahead.

Eventually arriving at RAF Bunchrew after 16 hours travelling, I was greeted enthusiastically at the main gate with the words, "Oh Christ, not another bloody one." It appeared I was not the only one having been sent to Bunchrew,

Invernesshire, instead of somewhere in Aberdeenshire. I was the fourth and last one to arrive that day. Bunchrew was a small camp and they did not like gatecrashers, hence the far from welcoming reception we received. They intended to kick us out as quickly as possible – and they did.

It was amongst the other three airmen who were stranded with me at Bunchrew that I met Tony Sinclair. Although I was to spend only a few weeks with Tony, I have never forgotten him. Having also taken the MT driving course at Weeton, Tony had been only the second trainee on record to have passed with the rank of Leading Aircraftsman. An extremely handsome looking chap and well spoken, Tony claimed that before joining the RAF he had been a playboy in London, supported by rich society women. Whether his stories were true or false, Tony was certainly a personality.

Within twelve hours of our arrival at Bunchrew, the four of us were bundled into the traditional 3-ton Bedford wagon and taken to Inverness railway station, put on a train to Aberdeen and told not to return. Arriving at Aberdeen we were transported to a mansion at Maryculter on the outskirts of the city, owned by a wealthy businessman, doing his little bit for 'King and Country' by accommodating nomadic RAF personnel nobody appeared to want.

Met at an imposing front door by the housekeeper – a stern, formidable figure – we were taken to the kitchen to be introduced to the cook and serving maid. The unshakeable living standards of the upper class still existed in wartime Britain. Then a climb up three flights of narrow back-stairs to a windowless attic room, just big enough for four iron camp beds. In such a stately mansion, I had been expecting a four-poster bed.

We were politely ordered by the housekeeper to take a bath, after which we would be taken to meet the Master or Laird, or whatever the Scottish gentry called themselves North of the Border. Baths taken, enough water for all four of us cramped into one bath, we were then escorted in single file by the housekeeper and ushered into a large room, where the 'fine old Scottish gentleman' was seated comfortably before a roaring fire, smoking a Churchillian-size cigar and drinking his 'wee dram'. The room was congested with antique furniture – a large dining table, dominated by a larger sideboard, displaying a collection of silverware, and cabinets overflowing with treasured china and glassware. The walls were covered by presumably priceless oil paintings and tapestries. We let Tony do the talking, after all he claimed he was a self-styled Lord. The audience did not last long. We quietly made our way out, leaving the old boy to reflect on his highland memories.

Next came a conducted tour of the house. My most memorable recollection was of an impressive hallway with a wrought iron staircase curving up to a circular gallery, the walls displaying more paintings. High above on the ceiling, a beautiful painting of the Madonna and child looked down on you. The housekeeper explained that the original owner of the house had commissioned an Italian artist to paint the work. When completed, the house owner complained he was dissatisfied with the painting and the artist became so distraught he committed suicide. The painting remained.

After the tour we were returned to the kitchen and deposited with the cook, I still remember that Sunday evening meal – curry, I did not like it then and I do not like it now. Having dined, I had eaten the curry, the cook made sure I did, we were let loose on the city with strict orders from the housekeeper to behave ourselves and not be back late – I had forgotten that I was in the RAF!

That first night in Aberdeen was a Sunday night. Getting off the bus in Aberdeen city centre, we went eagerly looking for a pub only to be told they were closed on Sunday, so off to find a cinema – they were also closed. Four despondent airmen on a cold and wet early December Sunday night, walking up and down Union Street, when one of the lads suggested going to church – we nearly shoved him under a bus!

Arriving at Burton's corner, three girls were standing in the shop doorway sheltering from the rain. Telling them our tale of woe, we were invited to their home. Life suddenly became more cheerful and realising we could be onto a good thing, we did not hesitate to accept their invitation. We were taken to an old tenement block of flats where, on entering, we were greeted by mother, father and two brothers sat around a table playing cards, a crate of bottled beer on the floor. Treated to genuine Scottish hospitality, we played cards with them and drank their beer, then given supper and sent back to our stately home. I have written that there were no pubs open in Aberdeen on a Sunday night – three months later my last night in the city was also a Sunday and we finished up as drunk as lords! It was just a case of knowing your way around.

We stayed at the mansion for two days, being fed two breakfasts of porridge and toast and two evening meals of curry. Supplied with vouchers for our lunch-time meals, where at a nearby cafe we dined on beans on toast. That was really high living.

After leaving the mansion, Tony Sinclair and I reported to a small radar station perched on a hill above the village of Balmedie, ten miles out on the coast road from Aberdeen to

Peterhead. The MT section consisted of three vehicles, two 15cwt Bedfords and a 3-ton Fordson.

After being at the camp a week, orders came through for a vehicle to go to London to collect some radar spares, Tony was given the job, to be accompanied by a second driver. He asked for me, but his request was refused, being told that he had to take a trainee driver with him, as a qualified driver could not be spared. Most RAF stations had trainee drivers, these were men who had re-mustered from one trade to another. Instead of going to a training school, they were trained by qualified drivers. Two years later, I was to be deeply indebted to one of these trainee drivers.

Tony set off on his long journey. Approaching London in the dark, he had stopped to check his route when a lorry ran into the rear of his vehicle. Tony received severe facial injuries, the trainee driver also sustained facial injuries but only minor. Tony was detained in a London hospital for 8 weeks. He returned to Balmedie just before I was posted away. His face was badly disfigured and he was partially blind in one eye. He continued to drive although I believed he should have been discharged and he probably was eventually. The story went around that Tony had jilted his fiancée, a London society girl (I did not know he had one) and proposed to the nurse who had looked after him during his stay in hospital.

The commanding officer at Balmedie was a young American Army Air Force officer posted to Britain to study radar. He was billeted in a private cottage in the village. I got involved in an amusing incident with this officer, at least he got involved with me.

There were not many local girls, but one of them, Maggie McCulloch, considered herself the 'belle' of the village. Maggie was very keen on one of the lads at the camp. I had been detailed to go and collect the commanding officer from his billet. As I sat in the cab waiting for him, Maggie walked up to my wagon. Opening the door to speak to her, she asked me if I had seen the lad she was keen on, I replied that he had just gone down the road with her one and only rival. In a fit of temper she let fly at me, I lost my grip on the door and fell out of the cab just in time for the commanding officer to see me hit the floor. He gently lifted me up and put me back into the driving seat. He could not resist a smile whenever we met after that.

Among the personnel at Balmedie were four WAAF radar operators, billeted (for sleeping purposes only) in the church manse on the edge of the village. Little was seen of them apart from the times they were collected and transported to their duties or in the dining room at meal times. Their main complaint being that before leaving the manse each morning, the parson would conduct a short prayer service for them. It was fortunate it was the Church of Scotland because if it had been Catholic they would have had to make their confessions and been at the manse all day.

The dining area on the camp at Balmedie was very small, the kitchen smaller. In charge of the two man staff was Corporal Alfie Turner, a good cook and a likeable chap. Alfie was almost a nervous wreck and had good cause to be. Since joining the RAF, Alfie's wife, Dolly, had followed him all over Britain, staying close to whichever camp he had been stationed.

At Balmedie, Dolly had found accommodation with an old couple in a cottage in the village. Being of a cantankerous nature, she was involved with daily arguments with the couple. They obviously tolerated her for the money she was paying.

After an argument, Dolly would make straight for the camp to vent her feelings on Alfie.

As soon as she was seen trekking up the lane that led to the camp, there would be a mad dash to the cookhouse to warn Alfie, who would be pushed into a small cupboard. Informing her that Alfie had gone out for supplies, Dolly would say, "I'll wait for him," and sit down on a stool. With Alfie sweating it out in the cupboard and the lads getting hungry, we could be ages persuading her to go, with the promise of letting her know when Alfie had returned to camp.

We were supplied with bath tokens and on Saturday afternoons we went into Aberdeen to the slipper baths for our weekly scrub-down. Not having to be back at camp until Sunday morning, we hit the town at night often frequenting a dockside pub. On one of these Saturday night jaunts, I was not only involved in a fight, but actually started it. The beer was flowing, the place full of RAF and Royal Navy, Army and Merchant Navy personnel. A girl sitting with a soldier stood up and started to sing, or to really describe it, screech. I told her to put a sock in it. Her soldier friend took a swipe at me and missed. My mates sensing trouble dragged me away. We ran down the stairs and outside on to the dockside. Looking back and gazing up at the building, there was one hell of a battle going on inside the building, with the sound of breaking glasses and windows being shattered. We put that place out of bounds and never returned, there were plenty of other pubs.

After finishing drinking on those Saturday nights, we made our way to a hostel for the Armed Forces. This place would be better described as a tramps den, where we ate stale meat pies, drank sludge classified as tea, then slept with our clothes and boots on so they did not get pinched. There was a similar place in Piccadilly in Manchester where I once stayed the night.

It was during this period that I spent my first Christmas and New Year in the RAF – 1942, the year Bing Crosby's song "I'm dreaming of a White Christmas" was first recorded. On Christmas Day morning with Balmedie covered in a thick white frost, we strolled to the local pub where the villagers made us welcome. After two pints of McEwans Strong Ale, we swayed merrily back to camp for Christmas dinner. Returning to the pub at night, the landlord put on a party for us. This was followed by New Years Eve (Hogmanay) and nobody can celebrate this festivity like the Scottish. Going into Aberdeen, people dragged us into their houses to celebrate with them. Whisky galore came out, food in abundance, including haggis, which they insisted we eat – and enjoy! I slept under somebody's sideboard that night, I wonder who they were?

One Saturday, I was given the duty of driving the liberty truck, a special wagon laid on for any personnel wishing to go into Aberdeen for the night. The return journey was along 10 miles of dark winding roads. Having had too much to drink, and driving a 3-ton wagon full of happily drunken airmen who were encouraging me to chase rabbits, I amazingly managed to get back to camp safely. Going later into Aberdeen in daylight and seeing the bends I had taken the previous night taught me a lesson I never repeated.

Another of our duties was to collect food supplies from Dyce Aerodrome on the outskirts of Aberdeen. During one of these trips, my wagon broke down and a mechanic from the main garage came out to repair the fault. The mechanic, Taffy Austin, was eventually posted to the camp where I was later stationed on the Shetland Isles. Taffy and I became very good friends.

I witnessed an unusual daily wartime occurrence, which took place at Dyce Aerodrome each evening at dusk. A passenger plane carrying businessmen, it's navigation lights on, would take off for Stockholm, the capital of Sweden. Being a neutral country, the plane had the freedom of the skies. They hopefully prayed they would not be shot down.

I had on one occasion to go to RAF School Hill, a large camp on the other side of Aberdeen for supplies. After having loaded my wagon and before returning to Balmedie, I went into the NAAFI and while trying to chew my way through one of their famous rock buns, a shadow loomed over the table. I looked up into the face of an SP – Service Policeman. He asked me if I was Jack Hambleton, I replied, "Yes." He said he was my cousin Harry, I did not recognise him, I had not seen him for years. He had seen my name in the guardroom arrival book when I had booked in. We had quite a conversation, a crowded canteen looking on with suspicion at my fraternising with a Service Policeman. These personnel were not exactly the Air Forces favourites.

Our Harry was later to create a spot of trouble for me on the Shetland Islands, but not as much as he created for himself back at School Hill. On a later visit that I made and in the same NAAFI, there was only one topic of conversation. An SP and a WAAF while dallying on some rocks had become stranded and cut off by the incoming tide, having to be rescued. Yes, it was Our Harry.

Balmedie was a good posting and Aberdeen a nice city with friendly people, but it was not to last. The only complaint I had was that the small station did not have a NAAFI so what chance had I of acquiring a jar of BRYLCREEM? I was beginning to lose faith in my keeping up the image of being a BRYLCREEM Boy! I felt I was letting the service down.

In early February 1943, I was called into the camp office and informed by the corporal clerk I was to be posted to the Shetland Islands. He told me the Shetlands was classified as an overseas posting and no member of the services could be sent there under the age of nineteen. I had another five weeks to go before reaching that age. He explained that if I wanted to object to the posting I could. Being fond of Balmedie and Aberdeen, I objected, but it was turned down. The reason given was that the posting was to be a temporary one, for only two weeks. This temporary posting became fifteen months. I was informed I was the youngest airman on record to be sent to the Shetlands, but that did not give me much satisfaction and once again, I was travelling alone.

CHAPTER THREE

SURE, A LITTLE BIT OF SHETLANDS

I travelled by train from Aberdeen to Invergordon, then by boat to Lerwick, the capital of the Shetlands. Of Invergordon I have two recollections. Firstly, it was a temperance town, no pubs or drinking of alcohol permitted, but with the speed they put me on the boat it did not matter. The other recollection was an impressive one.

In the middle of the Loch were anchored six large RAF Coastal Command Sunderland flying boats, surrounded by ten smaller Catalina flying boats. I was to later see these planes regularly flying low over the sea passing the Shetlands on their way to missions into German occupied Norway.

The boat trip was not exactly a leisure cruise. We sailed from Invergordon with a Royal Naval escort, an ancient ex-American destroyer, one of fifty commissioned during World War One, put into mothballs for 22 years, then 'lend/leased' to the British Government. The Yanks must have been delighted to get rid of these 'tin cans'. With thick clouds of smoke pouring out of the escort vessel's four funnels as it circled our boat, we did not know if it was putting out a smoke screen or the bloody thing was on fire. If we had been captured, the Germans would have thought they had a load of black faced natives.

The troopship was a filthy, rusty tub. The meals on board would not have been dished out in a workhouse. As a crowd of hungry men jostled around a dirty wooden table, a large greasy metal container full of cold, fat bacon and stale bread was flung at us, with a "Come and get it, you lucky lads!" Fortunately, no one was injured in the stampede but the slowest starved. I did not. That blasted assault course at Skegness was tame stuff compared to this.

We saw land in the distance and thinking it was the Shetlands, we shouted up to the Captain, "Can't you see that bloody land?" We were assured by a sailor that the land we were passing was the Fair Isles and not to be so eager as we would eventually get there. We did. Approaching Lerwick, I got my first glimpse of the Shetland Isles, an island where there was still a very strong Viking connection. An island of no pubs, no trees and very few girls and those were spoken for, but plenty of sheep. As my two weeks posting turned out to be fifteen months, I was to see plenty of them.

My new camp, Noss Hill, was a small radar station perched on the side of a steep hill reached only by a cart track. There was not a NAAFI, but a nearby camp, Watts Ness, about one mile away from Noss Hill possessed one. On the first night, I walked to Watts Ness and as had become my custom on arriving at a new posting, I asked in a hushed voice optimistically for a jar of BRYLCREEM and as I pessimistically expected, got a jar of bloody Anzora instead.

Noss Hill camp was so small that not only did it not possess a NAAFI, it did not even have a cook-house or dining room. We had to trail up to Watts Ness for our meals. There was one good arrangement. After each evening meal, we were supplied with food to cook for our breakfasts. With the bacon they supplied and the eggs we bought off the crofters, we did not do too badly. Our laundry was sent to Lerwick, but it took such a long time to be returned that washing clothes became another of our chores.

The RAF is the only branch of the armed forces where you cannot form long friendships. In the Army, soldiers move about together in regiments. In the Royal Navy, sailors serve together as a ship's crew. In the RAF, you are mainly posted alone. I experienced this during the whole of my four and a half years service.

Shortly after my arriving at Noss Hill, Taffy Austin, the mechanic who had repaired my wagon near Dyce Aerodrome at Aberdeen, also arrived at the camp. Taffy and I became close friends. As I was hopeless at cooking, he cooked my breakfast, I was also useless at washing clothes, this was proved when I boiled a pair of woollen socks, which came out of the tub resembling edible blue spaghetti, so Taffy helped me out with my laundry.

'Taffy' Austin

Noss Hill overlooked a Loch with the odd crofters cottages scattered along the waters edge. On the far side of the Loch in the distance rose a high mountain, Scousburgh. Perched precariously on the top of Scousburgh, it's tall mast often covered by cloud or mist, stood a radar station, staffed by technicians from

NO BRYLCREEM - NO MEDALS

our camp, working two 12-hour shifts. We were responsible for transporting these radar crews morning and night, a duty detailed on a rota system. There was not a tarmac road up the mountain, just a deep rutted track and driving a 3-ton Fordson wagon up there was no easy task, especially in bad weather.

One trip I have never forgotten occurred on a wild, cold and stormy night. With a 95 mph gale blowing, four men were on board ready to go up on duty, their mates at the top, waiting to come down and the track a gushing waterfall, I had somehow to get up there. When the wagon's front wheels became embedded in the mud I could not go forward. Turning the vehicle round, I reversed up the track from the bottom to the top. Two of the lads were outside at the rear guiding me, while the other two lay down in the back of the wagon acting as ballast. Reaching the radar station, the two poor devils who had been outside were soaked to the skin, shattered and still having a twelve-hour shift to work. I thanked God that I did not have to reverse down on the return trip, I just skidded down hoping for the best. There were other bad runs later on the same journey, but that night was the worst one.

During winter the weather was so cold that when setting off, my headgear was a balaclava helmet, my hands covered with woollen mittens and leather driving gloves. A greatcoat over a thick jersey and my trouser legs were encased with sea-boot stockings and gumboots. It was a struggle to get into the cab of the wagon. No wonder we were called the scruffy MT! The most satisfying part of this journey in winter was being given a generous tot of rum before setting off. It was in connection with this particular duty that I was later placed on a charge. The only charge I was to receive during my service life and that had an amusing side to it.

The Shetland Isles were a lonely, desolate place. In summer it rarely went dark and we could view the Northern Lights, a kaleidoscope of merging colours shining at their brilliant best. An unforgettable spectacle creating a picture no artist could paint. During the night's twilight, unable to sleep, we would wander along the cliff ridges, looking at a host of different types of sea birds. Other evenings, on a small sandy beach we played football or beachcombed amongst debris washed up on the shore from sunken ships. During the long winter nights when gales and storms of hurricane force raged, unless on duty, we stayed in the billet, not walking up to Watts Ness. In the winter, daytime rarely became light.

Driving lorries on twisting narrow roads no wider than English lanes, eyes would be strained to the far distance for glimpses of vehicles coming towards you, then trying to judge where you would meet them. One Army lorry careered off the road, plunging over the cliffs into the sea and a number of soldiers lost their lives.

After being in the service for over ten months, I was granted my second leave. To be going home even made that damn boat trip seem like a cruise, but with a long train journey following and taking almost two days to arrive home and two days to get back, the ten days leave became six days.

Entering wartime Sheffield by train and seeing barrage balloons suspended over the city was an impressive sight, until you realised why they were there.

I had been corresponding with two girls. As was the craze at the time, I had given them photographs of myself. They met purely by chance, as complete strangers, in the British Restaurant at the City Hall, proudly showing each other their pin-up who turned out to be the same lad! How I would have

An RAF Catalina flying boat on duty in the Shetlands, 1942.

liked to have been looking over their shoulders. I arrived on this leave jilted and lovelorn and spent it pub-crawling.

An amusing incident did occur. A pal serving in the Army was also on leave. While in the most exclusive of city pubs, the Barley Corn, the barmaid asked George, who was of small stature if he was eighteen years of age. Considering he was in Army uniform, her request was not very tactful. I had to restrain George from climbing over the bar counter to reach her. He almost started one of the famous wartime Battles of the Barley Corn, of which there were many. I had the pleasure of taking part in one on a later leave. Those six days at home soon passed and I was on my way back to the Shetlands.

We had very little to do with the Shetlanders. Although British by birth, they were still proud of their Nordic descent. We bought eggs from the crofters, which they packed for us to send home. Of all the dozens of eggs I sent, only one was received cracked. One of the lads, a Scotsman, received a bottle of whisky from his family. It arrived smashed to bits. We spent the evening chewing pieces of whisky sodden cardboard. Tasted nice, but was very tough to chew!

Jim (Spiv) Rodgers, a cockney, had a good arrangement with the local crofters. He would purchase from them sheep fleeces at five shillings each and post them off to his brother, who had a stall in London's Petticoat Lane. They must have been making a fortune until the crofters got wise to the racket and raised the price. Jim complained that the crofters were very hard businessmen to deal with!

Walking into the dining room at Watts Ness one day, I was greeted like a long lost brother by a happy, smiling Alfie Turner, the corporal cook who had been at Balmedie when I was stationed there. Asking him why he was so happy, Alfie said that at long last he had got away from his wife, Dolly, who had followed him from camp to camp wherever he had been stationed. I had last seen Dolly at Balmedie

The following week, going into the dining room, Alfie was sat with his head in his hands moaning and groaning. As I stood in front of him, he looked up and said to me, "Bloody Dolly's arrived, Hamby, she's in Lerwick!" Within a week, Dolly was installed in a Crofter's cottage about two miles away from the camp. While he walked to see her most nights, she kept away from the camp.

One of the main problems with RAF motor transport was the unsatisfactory condition of its vehicles. The Army and the shore based Royal Navy were supplied with new vehicles, while the RAF got the oldest and most were mechanically unreliable. They were rarely replaced and spares for existing vehicles difficult to come by.

Driving into Sumburgh aerodrome one morning, my wagon broke down on the airfield perimeter, the problem a leaking radiator causing water to drip on to the distributor. Taffy Austin came out and repaired it by plugging the leak with chewing gum out of his mouth. The chewing gum was still on that wagon's radiator when I left the Shetlands many months later.

The shortage of vehicle spares deteriorated to such an extent that 'Old Gricey', the sergeant in charge of maintenance, went over to the mainland to arrange for either decent vehicles or more spares. He was wasting his time, the condition of the vehicles never improved during the whole of my service days, no matter where I was stationed.

There were regular scares that a U-boat raiding party had landed on the island, especially on foggy days. One day I would drive into Sumburgh aerodrome and wave to the guards, the next day the same guards would stop me and search my wagon to check if I was hiding a U-boat crew.

One day, a local crofter out looking for a lost sheep spotted the wreckage of a crashed Halifax bomber at the foot of Fitful Head cliffs. The bomber, based in Scotland, had flown out to attack the German battleship, Tirpitz, sheltering in a Norwegian fjord. Due to severe stormy weather conditions, the Halifax crew had been unable to locate the Tirpitz. On the return flight the aircraft had crashed into the cliffs, within thirty feet of the top. An RAF Padre was lowered down the cliff face in a rope chair to conduct a service for the dead crew of five. Standing on the top of the cliff, we gazed down to pay our respects. The following day we were detailed to collect parts of the aircraft.

Then came the hilarious day when I was taken 'prisoner'. The powers that be decided that an exercise should be carried out to defend the camp against an enemy attack. The 'enemy' being a company of the KOSBI's (The Kings Own Scottish Border Infantry).

We took up our positions at ten o'clock on a Friday morning, crouching in ditches on a bleak windy hillside. All through the day we looked down into a valley, where on the other side another hill stretched up to the Fitful Head Cliffs. It appeared we were in an impregnable position. No enemy arrived. All through the following night, we strained our eyes into the darkness, being kept awake by the bleating of sheep. At ten o'clock the next morning, with everyone fast asleep from fatigue and frozen stiff, the 'enemy' attacked. I was roughly woken up. Standing over me, I was looking bleary eyed up the kilt of a rugged Scotsmen, his bayonet pressed against my throat, uttering the words, "Och, ye air mi' pris'ner."

Looking toward the makeshift cook-house, a large vat full of baked beans, which had been merrily bubbling away, now belched out clouds of thick black smoke, the 'enemy' having flung a smoke bomb into it.

It was decided at Watts Ness to have a feast. I cannot remember for what reason, possibly to drown the 'Shetland blues'. The corporal in charge of the cook-house, Bomber Lancaster, nicknamed after the famous heavy bomber, the Lancaster, suggested we club together and a sheep be bought from a nearby crofter. The crofter asked Bomber if he wanted the sheep dead or alive. Bomber said, "Alive, I'll kill it."

The whole camp assembled on the MT area to witness an event destined to be the RAF's answer to a Spanish Bullfight. To loud, enthusiastic cheering, 'Matador' Bomber appeared armed with an axe. The sheep was let loose and for twenty minutes he chased it, axe waving high – his face getting redder and gasping for breath, the axe getting lower. Bomber finally

NO BRYLCREEM - NO MEDALS

collapsed exhausted to the ground. The sheep, having stopped to look at Bomber sympathetically, was given to the crofter to kill and returned to us the following day ready for roasting and eating. It was suggested that the sheep should have been granted an RAF pardon.

Bomber was an amusing character. Every two weeks, a film show was held on the camp. We should have expected lantern slides, but the RAF were up-to-date, although the equipment used was so antique, the whirring of the projector drowned out the soundtrack of the film. Any films showing sea scenes and most of them did, made Bomber seasick and considering we were surrounded by the sea, it was hilarious. No one would tell Bomber what the film to be shown was about. He would sit on the front row and a sea scene would appear on the screen. Bomber would make a dash to the door where one of the lads was waiting to hand him a bucket. Bomber then vanished out into the night. When he was posted back to the mainland, they must have blindfolded him aboard the ship until he stepped ashore at Invergordon.

CHAPTER FOUR

THE 'JOSEFSKY STALINSKY'

hile at Noss Hill I was transferred twice, first to Lerwick, then to the island of Foula. At Lerwick, the RAF personnel were three – an officer, Ronnie Wilson and me. I was never quite sure what we were there for and we rarely saw the officer. I would drive the one and only vehicle, an old Standard van without brakes along the quayside, keeping well away from the edge of the water. At least the engine got a run, if not the brakes.

Ronnie and I slept in a small room over a fish-gutting warehouse on the dockside, we stank of dead fish, as did the girls who noisily worked there. We had our meals in a nearby Army dining hall.

Lerwick was a base for Norwegian motor torpedo boats. The crews operating these crafts, sailing into German occupied Norwegian waters, would return from action, occasionally badly shot up and we would assist in carrying both dead and wounded off the boats. These men sailed the famous Shetland Bus. Going out on their Patrols into German held waters, the MTB's crews would merge with the Norwegian fishing fleet and drop a colleague off disguised as a fisherman. After he had been home to see his family and also passed messages on to the families of other crew members, the MTB's would return to pick him up. I had a lot of admiration and respect for these fearless men.

The supply base for submarines, both British and Allied, was also at Lerwick. Strolling into the servicemen's canteen one evening with Ronnie Wilson, we walked straight into the middle of one of the toughest looking bunch of fellows I had ever seen. Twenty of them, members of the crew of the Russian submarine, the Josefsky Stalinsky, which had that morning sailed into Lerwick for supplies. They were being entertained by a lone British cockney soldier, who at five foot six was almost submerged by the brawny six-foot plus sailors.

Ronnie and I were dragged into the circle for a night of beer swilling and vodka drinking revelry. The Russians did not speak English, we did not speak Russian, but we all drank the same way. Beer and vodka flowed. They insisted on not merely touching glasses, but banging them together with every drink. Broken glasses and spilled beer and vodka covered the tables and the floor. I was seated, or squashed, between Ivan Borisovsky and Boris Ivanovsky. The Russians appear to be fond of using both Christian names and surnames, switching them about to save confusion, at least that was their theory. Swapping caps, I looked smarter in a soft round flat cap with a tassel down the back, which, although it came down to my ears, matched my tunic better than my Russian friend looked with an RAF forage cap on.

Out came photographs of their wives and girl friends, smiling, sturdily built Russian women. As the beer and vodka continued to swill around, one of the Russians who could only speak two words of English, "Vinshan Shirtil," which when translated meant Winston Churchill, was gesticulating with his arms. He eventually managed to suggest they teach us the

Russian National Anthem, providing we taught them the British National Anthem.

They applauded enthusiastically with much glass smashing as we stood in the middle of the room singing the 'Red Flag' and waving a flag complete with its hammer and sickle. The whole canteen was now singing. Having finished our rendering of their national anthem, they could not wait to learn ours. We taught them, "Jesus wants me for a sunbeam and a bloody fine sunbeam am I!" This became an immediate hit, with twenty deep bass Russian voices roaring *"Yesis vlants me flo ya shunbim yan ya bloo-oody fline shunbim yam yi!"*

Their singing of what they believed to be the British National Anthem has never been more passionately sung. The room rocked, the light fittings swayed, the bar ran out of glasses. The evening finished. We staggered out, arms round shoulders for support into an almost dark, clear starry night, making our way to the harbour and the Josefsky Stalinsky.

The following morning with heads that felt like blown up balloons and the pounding of giant hammers in our skulls, Ronnie Wilson and myself made our way along the quayside to the dining room in Brown's yard for breakfast, having to pass the Josefsky Stalinsky. We stopped, then decided to go up the gangplank to meet our pals of the previous night. Reaching the top, an officer and two sailors rushed towards us, their rifles pointing at our chests. We were dragged by the scruff of the neck along the gangway and arrested for spying. With our arms waving, we attempted to explain that we had called to see our new allies of the previous evening. The Russian officer pointed to the conning tower of the submarine, telling us in broken English that we were going to be chained there and when they sailed, should they have to submerge, it would be our rotten bloody luck!

Ronnie suggested to me we try to pacify them by singing the 'Red Flag'. We sang, the officer and guards standing to attention, looking on in amazement. Then, from down below in the boat came the sound of deep bass voices bellowing out, *"Yesis vlants me flo ya shunbim, yen ya bloo-oody fline shunbim yam yi."*

One of the Russians we had been drinking with the previous night came and spoke to the officer who, with a broad grin on his face, released his hold on us. We were then escorted from the submarine and into the dining room to make sure we did not return. We did not.

As we passed the Josefsky Stalinsky on our return from breakfast, the submarine was preparing to sail. I looked up at the conning tower and thought, "Christ, but for the grace of God, the 'Red Flag' and a lone Russian submariner, I could have been somewhere out at sea chained to that damn conning tower and feeding the fishes in Davy Jones Locker."

By this time I was getting fed up of being taken prisoner, first by our own forces and now by the Russians.

A British submarine, the Thunderbolt, sailed into Lerwick for supplies. This ship had been built before the war – as the Thetis – it had become famous through tragic circumstances. While undergoing sea trials in Liverpool Bay during the 1930s, the Thetis had submerged and failed to resurface, causing heavy loss of both service and civilian life. Having been recovered and refitted, it was commissioned and entered into Royal Naval Service as the Thunderbolt. We spent a wonderful evening with it's crew. The submarine departed the following morning and was sunk some days later with the loss of that crew.

One afternoon, I was strolling on a small beach outside Lerwick with Ronnie Wilson. A lady walking alone approached us. She stopped to talk and asked where our homes were. We told her, she smiled and wished us luck. As she walked away, she turned to wave. It was Gracie Fields, her popular song at the time was, 'Wish me luck as you wave me goodbye.' Which we did.

I moved from Lerwick, going to the island of Foula for fourteen days. The journey was on a beautiful summer evening. Sailing in a small, dirty coaster, the boat was crowded with crofters and pigs, poultry and nuns, in that order. The weather was as perfect as the scenery, which was breathtaking. As the boat moved between and stopped at small islands, the sun refused to go down.

Within a few days of returning to Noss Hill, I was placed on my one and only charge. This turned out to be more humorous than serious. The commanding officer had been invited to a Boat Night party, being held for an officer pal returning to the mainland. These events were held when anyone, irrespective of rank, was posted away from the Shetlands.

The camp where this party was to be held was on the other side of the island. After passing through Lerwick, it could only be reached along cart tracks. When the CO requested a driver to transport him, it was discovered that I was the only one who knew the way. There was a problem, it was my week to take those chaps up and down Scousburgh mountain. The CO ordered the MT corporal that I be relieved of this night run.

We drove to the Boat Night party in a 15 cwt Bedford, a junior officer riding in the back, the poor devil having the roughest ride of his life over the rocky cart tracks. Arriving at

NO BRYLCREEM - NO MEDALS

the camp, the CO left me in the cookhouse, ordering the cooks, "Look after him." While the party was in progress the CO came to see if I was OK, I was eating a whole chicken. Telling me I was being looked after better than he was, I gave him a leg of the chicken!

We left the party at two o'clock in the morning to return to Noss Hill. At such an early hour and pitch dark and the CO snoring at my side, it was more by luck than judgement that we arrived back at camp about 4.30 am. Getting the young officer out of the rear of the wagon, I found he had brought up everything he had eaten and drunk at the party. Having to swill out the back, I eventually got into bed at 5.30 am.

That was when the trouble started. Being due to take the morning shift of radar lads up the mountain at 8 am and bring the previous night shift down, I overslept and someone else had to do the run. The MT corporal, whom I had never got on well with, placed me on a charge. I was confined to camp for seven days, which on the Shetlands was not a punishment but a rest, then brought before the CO on a charge of being absent from my duties. He asked me my defence. I said I hadn't any and admitted oversleeping. With it being his fault, he appreciated my reply. He gave me a punishment of seven days confined to camp. Having already been confined to camp for seven days, I considered it an unfair punishment. A sentence of fourteen days would have meant another seven days rest.

As I saluted and turned round to walk out of his office, the CO winked. I doubt that had ever been done before or since. After the trial and up to the day I left the Shetlands, if the CO wanted a driver to transport him about, I had to take him. I did not mind, but what concerned me was he could have been responsible for me facing more charges. He was an interesting person. During our trips out he would talk about his life, having been a Welsh rugby international.

Live entertainment on the camp was rare, we appeared to be forgotten. An ENSA group did arrive one night and the acts were so bad that they mesmerised the audience into silence. The conjurer could not hold a pack of cards, let alone shuffle them; the singer forgot the words of the song 'Nellie Dean' and the chorus girls should have been drawing their old age pensions.

While the comedian was laughing at his own jokes to a bored audience, there was a sudden outburst of laughter and loud cheering. He looked at them with amazement and pride, believing he was about to become famous. The reason for the ovation was when he started to recite 'Twinkle, Twinkle Little Star.' Unknown to him, one of the camp's corporals was named Starr, with an obvious nickname of 'Twinkle'. Even 'Twinkle' saw the humorous side to it.

It was billed one night that we were to be entertained by the famous 'Tiny' Winters. Very few had ever heard of him, but to anyone familiar with the dance band scene, Tiny was indeed well known.

This particular night, the camp was being buffeted by a 90-mph gale. With a packed canteen and 'Tiny' well overdue, the chaps having waited patiently were singing, "Why are we waiting," from the carol, 'O Come All Ye Faithful'. Standing near the door, I went outside to see if 'Tiny' had arrived. As I walked into the dark, a small 5 foot 3 inches figure, struggling against the wind, carrying a 6-foot high double bass ran straight into me. As I sank to the ground, 'Tiny' walked straight over me. In spite of our unusual meeting, I must say 'Tiny' was the best turn we had up there.

NO BRYLCREEM - NO MEDALS

A new arrival at Noss Hill was a Geordie, Kenny Ashcroft. His first night in the billet, when he was getting the normal interrogation reserved for newcomers, he learned that I was from Sheffield. Kenny said his previous camp had been School Hill near Aberdeen, which I have mentioned earlier. He remarked that a service policeman stationed at School Hill was a Sheffield United footballer. I asked him the chap's name. When he told me, I replied that although the SP had the same name as a well-known Sheffield United footballer, the fellow had never kicked a football in his life, he was in fact my cousin. It was Our Harry.

Kenny insisted he was right and that I did not know what I was talking about. It almost turned into a roughhouse. During the time we were together Kenny and I really got on well, but he still insisted that Our Harry was a Sheffield United footballer.

During the long drawn out summer evenings, weather permitting and not on duty, Taffy Austin and I would walk the six miles round the Loch. We would talk about the past, our childhood days and our parents. We talked about the present and what the future possibly held. Taffy came from near Swansea and he spoke fondly of his mother who regularly wrote to him, I never heard him mention his father.

With service on the Shetlands being classified as an overseas posting, we were issued with a free allocation of fifty cigarettes a week. At the time I did not smoke. Going home on the two leaves I had while stationed there, I was able to take large amounts of cigarettes for my father, who obviously hoped I would remain there for the duration of the War.

One evening, one of the lads decided to have all his hair shaved off. Sitting him in the middle of the hut, we started with an old pair of scissors and finished the job off with a safety razor. He looked and felt a right berk. The following week he was posted back to the mainland.

The Shetlands tour of duty was supposed to be eighteen months, I had served thirteen months and was beginning to suffer from the dreaded 'Shetlanditis' (talking to the sheep). I did not relish another five months there, so I decided to re-muster, i.e. change trades. During my trips to Lerwick and Sumburgh, I had seen the Air Sea Rescue bases. Sailing around the waters in an Air Sea Rescue launch appeared to be a pleasant occupation. In fact, the Sumburgh launch crews were dab hands at fishing. I applied to re-muster for training as a fitter marine on a launch. I was not very optimistic of passing and within four weeks, I was on my way.

On my final night at Noss Hill, the traditional Boat Night party was held in the NAAFI at Watts Ness. The CO came, bought me a pint, regretted he could not get me on any more charges, slapped me on the back and wished me good luck. The Shetlands theme song was sung lustily to the tune of a well-known Irish Ballad…..

Sure a little bit of SHETLANDS fell from out the sky one day,
And it landed in the ocean many, many miles away,
And when the Air Force saw it, it looked so bloody bare.
They said that's what we are looking for, we'll send our airmen there.
So they built a couple of pylons and a Nissen hut or two,
Sent the boys from England, just to see what they could do,
And now they're bloody fed up, browned off and far from home,
And all you can hear them say is,
"ROLL ON THAT BLOODY BOAT!"

I was away, alone again, heading for Locking, near Weston-Super-Mare. The journeys seemed to get longer. I hoped that even if I did not make it as a fitter marine, I should be able to buy some BRYLCREEM – my hair still being plastered down with bloody Anzora.

RAF Locking was a large camp used for training mechanical trades. I arrived, along with twenty-nine others, all having re-mustered to get away from unpopular postings. The training course was for ten weeks, days spent with our heads in engineering manuals and filing pieces of metal. At the end of the course, out of the thirty hopefuls, only one passed and he had previous engineering experience. I met him three years later in Blackpool Tower.

Having flopped the fitter marine course and still unable to buy any BRYLCREEM, it was back to driving and I was on my way to the romantic town of Bolton in Lancashire. The RAF had quarters in the centre of town in a building that had previously been a college. I never bothered to find out what they were up to at Bolton, I was not to stay long enough, but I do recall their one and only vehicle was a Standard Van having no hand-brake. Not having a NAAFI, even the town's hairdressers did not have any BRYLCREEM. I was billeted with another lad in a small terraced house, with a homely, friendly Lancashire family. Our two iron camp beds were squeezed into a small attic. The daily menu never varied, a hot breakfast consisting of toast and jam, a hot evening meal of fish and chips from the corner shop.

CHAPTER FIVE

"BE'JAYSUS, THE BLOODY TENT'S ON FIRE!"

Leaving Bolton after three weeks and expecting leave but not getting any, I was on my way to Hatfield in Hertfordshire to join an Airfield Construction Unit. Life during the thirteen weeks since departing from the Shetlands had been peaceful. That was to change! The following five months were to be spent roaming around the South of England with the most extraordinary group of men I was to encounter, they could only be described as a gang of twenty Irish 'navvies' in RAF uniform.

My first meeting with them ended in total confusion. There were nine Murphys, three O'Flannagans, three O'Shaughnessys, two McGintys, one O'Neill and one Smith. How an Irishman came to be christened by the name of Smith I never discovered. I nicknamed him 'Geordie', a name that stuck. The remaining one, I never knew his name. He answered to the name of 'Marbles' and was the proud possessor of a glass eye. When I shouted Paddy, eighteen glaring faces turned towards me. When I shouted Geordie, or Marbles, the other two responded.

The MT section on this unit consisted of two troop carrier vehicles and four tippers. My vehicle, a Fordson Troop Carrier, the least said about the condition of this wagon the better. Old

Gricey, my old MT sergeant on the Shetlands would have deserted. Nicknamed by the gang as the 'six merry lads', we six drivers were to keep together for seven months, right up to arriving at a transit camp at Heliopolis on the outskirts of Cairo in Egypt before separating to go our different ways.

The duties of the Airfield Construction Unit were to arrive early morning at an airfield where repairs to the runways or perimeters were needed, remain until the work was completed, normally a few days, then move on. After getting the gang on to the job and apart from collecting materials I had little to do but hang around. These lads were workers who grafted hard during the day, but at night after a few drinks in the NAAFI, no one could control them. The first night we arrived at a station, a fight could be guaranteed. The next night, the NAAFI would be deserted by the station's personnel, leaving the gang to fight amongst themselves. The following morning, nursing a few aches, pains and bruises they were all once again bosom pals. While the fights were taking place, we six merry lads would walk away – much to their amusement, but we were accepted and well looked after by them.

One station we arrived at was an American Army Air Force Base at Ramsbury in Wiltshire, where we stayed for four weeks. After some of the places I had been to and was later to visit, this camp was a heavenly paradise. We were allowed to share the Americans facilities, including their living quarters. The Nissen huts were so well furnished that we considered them to be palaces of luxury.

On entering the dining hall for a meal, your hands were inspected by the duty officer. If dirty, you were despatched to the wash rooms and your hands again inspected on your return. The meals were wholesome and plentiful. After each man had been served his meal, the duty officer would receive the same food and sit amongst the men. No British Flight Sergeant bawling down the room, "Any complaints." Coming out of the dining room after having eaten the meal, three large zinc containers of water had been placed for the washing of your plates, one containing hot soapy water, one hot clear water and the remaining one cold clear water. Not, as on RAF stations where one tub of cold greasy water would be changed every Christmas Day. The American's strictness in hygiene was much to be admired.

We were permitted to use the American's leisure facilities and their PX. This building was equivalent to the British NAAFI canteen and there the similarity ended. We were issued with a card to purchase 200 cigarettes and half a pound of chocolate per week. Chewing gum was not rationed, as well as many other items unobtainable in wartime Britain. The personnel behind the counter were most apologetic when I asked for a jar of BRYLCREEM, wanting to know what it was for. They thought it was cream to put in coffee. Thankfully they did not sell bloody Anzora either. Only being paid a fraction of the money the Americans received, we could only look on with envy.

During our stay at Ramsbury, the gang behaved themselves impeccably, at least on the camp. We made friends amongst the Americans who came into our billet in the evenings. Many a constructive discussion with them took place. They were eager to know of our home towns and families.

On Saturday nights, I would drive the gang to Hungerford, where the locals had been advised to lock up their daughters and even their wives for the night. During one return journey, with the Irish Male Voice Choir in the back of the wagon

NO BRYLCREEM - NO MEDALS

rendering their own bawdy version of the song 'Danny Boy' and driving along a dark narrow lane, I spotted in the beam of my headlights an American. Stopping to pick him up, he turned out to be one of our 'evening' friends. He should have been back in camp some hours previously. If caught he would face a Court Martial. Smuggling him into the camp proved to be no problem. One of the Murphys stripped and putting his uniform on the GI, we got him back into the camp. The Yank even waved to the guards as I drove through the main gate.

The Americans had an unusual method of punishment for erring personnel. Their form of 'jankers' (RAF punishment) for a wrongdoer was to be sentenced to a number of days sweeping the runways and perimeters. While carrying out his punishment, the offender would have ten steps behind him, an armed guard. They could possibly be friends and most of the time would be swapping cigarettes and jokes.

Attached to Ramsbury was a British Army Glider Unit. One morning, having arrived on the airfield perimeter and unloaded the gang to start their work, an Army sergeant came over, asking if we wanted a flight in a glider. All tools were dropped and all wagons left as we piled into a Horsa glider. A dog, which was always hanging around because we fed it, also jumped in as a passenger.

The flight lasted thirty minutes. No seats, we just sat on the floor, the damn thing bumped and rocked all over the place. Having nothing to hang on to, we did the same. When the glider landed, we almost fell out of the hatch then swayed on the tarmac as if drunk. The dog jumped off and calmly ran away. The sergeant pilot came and thanked us for going with him, explaining that the glider had recently been fitted with a new tail-plane and wanting ballast, he thought we would give him the extra weight needed and enjoy the trip.

The following day while watching the gang toiling, I was standing close to a Dakota aircraft. As the pilot started up the plane's engines, I turned round to prevent the dust going into my eyes. The draught from the propellers caused a large, empty tar drum, which was lying on it's side to roll towards me, hitting me squarely on the back of both legs. The pain in my legs was so intense I thought I had broken them. I managed to drive to the American sick bay. After X-rays and treatment I was assured I had no injuries, apart from bad bruising. The medical officer discharged me, advising me to keep away from Dakotas in the future. Driving for the next few days became sheer agony.

Living and working in such pleasurable conditions, the gang tried to slow their work rate and make the job last out longer than it should take, but unsuccessfully.

We moved to a forest in West Sussex, which became our base. Life was rough and tough – small trees being chopped down to make beds. Each evening after parking my wagon I would drain the radiator – a queue of chaps waiting for the hot rusty water to have a shave.

Settling down to bed one night, Marbles complained of feeling cold. Being the brainiest one of the gang, he filled a paraffin stove with petrol. Lighting it, the resulting explosion sent the other five paddies in the tent dashing out, as naked as the day they were born, yelling, "Be'jaysus, the bloody tent's on fire!" An empty oil drum was attached to a hook on a tree to sound the alarm, in case of fire. Geordie Smith going to raise the alarm, clouted the drum with such force that it fell off the hook on to his foot and broke a toe. In the meantime, we had all dashed out from the other tents and were piling some of our well-worn dirty working clothes on to the fire, in the hope of being issued with new replacements. Having to take Geordie to Chichester Hospital for treatment to his foot, we did not return until the early hours of the morning. Everyone was still milling around with laughter echoing through the forest.

It appeared that Marbles, when he went to bed at night, always put his glass eye in his tunic pocket. Having thrown the tunic on the fire, the glass eye had gone with it. When daylight arrived and the fire was out, a sifting operation began through the cooled ashes for Marbles glass eye. Unable to find it, I had another trip to Chichester Hospital, this time taking Marbles for a new glass eye. Being unable to supply him with one immediately, we returned to the forest, Marbles wearing a black patch. For the next three weeks he was nicknamed Pirate Pat. A more serious problem then arose, resulting from having thrown our clothes on the fire. It was three weeks before we received replacements, so we were stuck with only one set of working togs.

I would go to a depot near Chichester to collect rolls of Summerfield Tracking, a form of steel netting, returning for the gang to lay it in strips on flat fields, which became temporary runways for Spitfires and Hurricanes to operate from.

On our return to the forest one evening, four Spitfires flew over in single file, a formation used by pilots when returning to base having been on a sortie. The leading plane's engine appeared to stall, the second plane in attempting to avoid it clipped the leader's tail-plane causing the plane to dive into the forest, the second plane crashing some distance away behind the local pub. Loading my wagon with fire extinguishers, I drove on a track through the forest under the overhanging tree branches, smashing the wooden frame and ripping the canvas tarpaulin covering the back of the wagon.

We reached the Spitfire, which had crashed through tall trees and embedded itself in the ground. Fortunately, it had not caught fire. At first we could see no sign of the pilot, then one of the lads spotted something suspended from a tree branch. It was the pilot, his parachute half open, the poor devil was completely cut in half, the upper part of his body still in the tree, the lower half on the ground. He had attempted to bale out, but too late. Wrapping what we could of him in his parachute, an ambulance arrived, having also got through the forest. We were later informed the pilot of the other plane that crashed had died on his way to hospital.

Returning to camp, because of the rough ground, all the fire extinguishers had discharged in the back of the wagon, flooding it with foam. Parking the vehicle and cleaning it out, the commanding officer, a South African, came up to me. He told me not to fill an accident report in or worry about the damage to the framework, I had done a wonderful job and no disciplinary action would be taken against me. It was the only time during my service career I did any damage to a vehicle. Until the damaged parts were replaced, the gang travelled draughty and cold.

During one night, a German bomber flew over the forest and 'bombed' us with thousands of strips of silver paper. These were designed to put the country's radar systems out of action. Packed in large bundles, they should have opened before they hit the ground, some did, some did not and we could only thank God it was silver paper and not bombs they had dropped.

Clean clothes were our biggest problem. We had to wash some ourselves and the others were sent to a laundry in

Chichester. The laundry having had one batch for over two weeks and with no sign of them being returned, the commanding officer rang the laundry enquiring when they would be ready. He was told, the following day. I was detailed to go into Chichester and collect it. During that afternoon, an American Liberator bomber returning from a raid over Germany, crashed onto the laundry killing the plane's crew and also a number of the laundry workers. We had to continue wearing mucky gear.

I then had a stroke of good fortune. Some nights we walked to the nearest town, Emsworth, three miles away, to go to a cinema. I met a girl who took me home to meet her parents. Feeling sorry for me, her mother started to wash my clothes. They had another daughter living at home, married to a Flight Sergeant with a cushy posting at nearby Thorney Island. I would borrow his shirts, I doubt whether he ever knew, in fact I never met him. They also supplied me with an old push-bike so I could ride between Emsworth and the camp. This was a marvellous arrangement until the girl got serious. I then transferred her and the bike to one of my mates. He was happy, he got his washing done and could cycle to town. I had to go back to wearing mucky clothes and walking.

About three weeks after Marbles had thrown his glass eye on the fire, the CO received a telephone call from Chichester Hospital advising him that a replacement eye could be collected. Taking Marbles, who was fed up with the black eye patch he had been wearing, I did not realise what I was letting myself in for and how embarrassing it would be. A doctor fitted the new glass eye into Marbles empty eye socket, stood back to admire his work and asked him how he felt. "OK," said Marbles, "but be'jaysus, I can'na see through it!"

The doctor replied, "Don't be so daft, man, you can't see through a glass eye." With which Marbles said, "I could with the last one!" The doctor looked at me, saying, "Take him away, or I will have him put away!" I dragged a protesting Marbles out of the hospital and into my wagon.

A major problem we experienced was pay. We never knew how or when we would be paid or, how much money we would receive when eventually paid. Not only were my mates and I unhappy about the situation, there was a lot of muttering going on between the two gangs.

One morning, we six merry lads went to the clearing where the wagons were parked, to check them over. The tippers had departed and 'Vicky' Vickers and I waited for the gangs to arrive. With no sign of our passengers, we returned to the camp. We found them grouped and noisily arguing among themselves. They told us they would not be going out that day, they were going on strike until their pay problems were sorted out to their satisfaction. I pointed out to them that their action would not be regarded as a strike, but as a mutiny, which was the most serious crime to be committed in the armed forces. They would all be lined up and in the peace of an English forest, blindfolded and shot by a firing squad.

Becoming calmer, one of the paddies suggested that as I was the 'blue-eyed boy' of the officer in charge, because when I had damaged my wagon going through the forest to the crashed Spitfire, the officer had patted me on the back, I should negotiate with him on their behalf. I went to see the officer, explaining the position. I also mentioned to him about my warnings to the men of their possible executions by a firing squad. Not only was this particular officer one of the best I had served under, he was a man with a great sense of humour.

Returning with me, he told the gangs that if they were prepared to trust him, he would get their pay problems sorted out, otherwise he would have no alternative but to send for the firing squads. Knowing of the sense of humour these Irish lads possessed, the situation became light-hearted.

Two days later, the officer told me he had arranged for me to go to the RAF Station at Thorney Island, near Chichester and collect a pay clerk, who would return with me, meet the men, discuss and hopefully sort out their problems. Arriving at the accounts section at Thorney Island, I was surprised to find the pay clerk I was to transport was a very attractive WAAF corporal. I thought when the men see this one, they will forget their grievances. They did.

Amid the tents, trees and twittering birds and sitting on a tree trunk at a makeshift table, she discussed with each man his pay and with a smile and a promise said, "It will be sorted out." She kept her word. By the weekend an officer came out and paid each and every one of us what we were entitled to.

When I had picked the WAAF corporal up at Thorney Island and during the journey to camp, she told me she was married to the sergeant in charge of the pay unit and they were living in a flat in Chichester. Returning with her to Chichester, she told me to take her to the flat, where she expected her husband to be there preparing a meal for us.

CHAPTER SIX

DODGIN' DOODLEBUGS

At the side of the forest stood a large imposing mansion, Stansted House. One sunny Sunday morning, the owner, the Earl of Bessborough, wandered into the camp asking to speak to the officer in charge. The Earl requested from him, "Could you pick eleven men to play my team at cricket?"

Duly obliging, we made our appearance on what the Earl boasted to be the 'Lords' of West Sussex. We were supplied with cricket gear, but still looked like a troupe of clowns from Chipperfields Circus. Being gentlemen, the Earl's team put us in to bat first.

I was 'press-ganged' to open the innings. Their fast bowler, the estate's Head Gardener, came pounding in at what seemed to be a hundred miles an hour. I stood there mesmerised, shaking in the ill-fitting pads. The first ball glanced off the edge of my bat, flying to the boundary for four runs, cheers erupted from the gang who were stood on the boundary, I proudly raised my bat in acknowledgement.

The bowler walked down the wicket, face to face he looked glaringly at me, then returned to his starting mark, vigorously rubbing the ball down the side of his white flannels. Roaring in for his second delivery, the ball missed me, missed the bat and hit the middle stump with such force it almost went to the boundary. The others came in and went out, enjoying every minute of the match. We were trounced, but not disgraced.

After the match had ended, the Earl, his Countess and family came out from the house carrying silver teapots and trays, laden with plates of cucumber sandwiches to be eaten while we sat on their immaculate lawn. The gang, whom I had never seen so genteel, spent the afternoon hobnobbing with the aristocracy – although I noticed one or two of them had their eyes firmly fixed on the silverware!

Taking the gang to an airfield near Chichester one morning, I was given a further call to make near the town centre to collect equipment. Arriving in what appeared to be the play-yard of an infants school, a WAAF officer came out asking me not, "What do you want" but "What are you doing here?"

Ordering the lot of us out of the wagon, we were taken into the building. I had driven by mistake into the Headquarters of the Area Fighter Command Operations.

The walls of the old classroom were covered with large maps, high stools were placed around wide tables seating

Stansted House, West Sussex.

WAAF's, who were studiously shuffling model aeroplanes around with long sticks. There was complete silence, then their sticks clattered to the floor as they gazed with open mouths, never having seen such a scruffy lot of individuals. Knowing the gang chased every bit of skirt they looked at, my heart was in my mouth.

We were lined up like a group of naughty schoolboys in front of a high-ranking officer, who with a wagging of his finger, warned us we could be arrested for spying. He then ordered us to keep quiet about what we had seen and sent us on our way.

That day was full of surprises. On our way back to the forest, we came upon an American GI thumbing a lift. Picking him up, he spoke with a perfect cockney accent, explaining he had been a sailor in the British Merchant Navy, sailed to America and joined their army. He paid for his lift with chewing gum.

The time came to move out of the area and with no regrets, we left the forest. Germany had started their flying bomb – Doodlebug – attacks on London so we headed for Kent. The Fordson trooper was left behind and in it's place I was supplied with an American left-hand drive Studebaker. It was the best wagon I had driven, or was to drive, during the remainder of my service days.

In the Fordson trooper the gang had spent their travelling time sat on rickety forms playing cards, I would regularly brake sharply, scattering them all over the rear of the vehicle. This new vehicle had fixed seats. When I now braked sharply, they stayed put, blowing out loud raspberries.

Before arriving in Kent, we called at a Barrage Balloon Unit near Southampton to pick up an officer. We had to stay the night and what a night it turned out to be.

Sensing there would be trouble, we six merry lads went to the camp cinema. There were two gangs of twenty men, the gang I tried to control, the other lot Vicky Vickers was lumbered with. As predicted they went wild, wrecking the NAAFI. The WAAF's had to be locked up for their own safety. We could hear the pandemonium raging outside the cinema. We honestly believed this was it, they would all get locked up and we would never see Kent. The amazing thing was, they never got into trouble, only created it. All camps welcomed us, but no camp waved us goodbye.

Reaching Kent, we were to be on the move all the time, the officer in charge receiving his instructions daily. We would make our way into narrow country lanes and locate a field, which to the officer was a cross on his map. The gang would then build a concrete base for a cable winch and by the evening a crew had arrived and a barrage balloon would be flying. Every barrage balloon in the country was brought into this area, some from as far away as Glasgow, it was a fantastic operation.

The main problem to be encountered was Doodlebugs having flown across the Channel, they had reached their maximum height over Kent. As we gazed up, these carriers of death were flying over the top of the barrage balloons, with fighter planes pursuing them, their pilots having to be watchful of getting entangled in the winch cables.

One of the most gratifying moments was watching a Typhoon fighter tip the small wing of a Doodlebug, turning it around and sending it back to where it had come from. One of the saddest, when a Doodlebug having lost height, flew into and spiralled down a winch cable, killing two of the barrage balloon crew.

Travelling in convoy one sunny Sunday evening, we stopped in the main street of Sevenoaks in Kent. The local people came out of their houses carrying trays loaded with pots of tea and buns to welcome us, it had the atmosphere of a street party.

For the public to see an Airfield Construction Unit on the move must have been one of the most morale boosting spectacles of the war. The tipper wagons led the way, overflowing with kit bags and home-made beds, field kitchens and spades, pick axes and wheelbarrows. The troop carriers followed loaded with gangs of boisterous Irishmen, singing and whistling to the girls by the wayside. We were always loudly cheered on our way by bystanders when passing through towns and villages.

Stopping in Ashford in Kent, we had gone into a WRVS canteen. Returning to my wagon, an old, creased brown envelope had been placed under the windscreen wiper, with these simple words written on it – *To all you boys in Air Force Blue, God Bless You* – I wondered who the person was who wrote those few words of blessing.

This period was hectic, I never knew which was the most dangerous, dodging Doodlebugs or trying to keep the gang out of trouble. Amongst the civilians they were well behaved, it was only when we arrived on camps they went wild. In the pubs we visited, we were usually treated to plenty of beer.

In one pub in Ashford one night, a couple sitting in the middle of us said they lived in the house next door. I told them we drove past every morning at 7.30 am. They asked me to blow the vehicle hooter to wake them up. During the following week, all six wagons blew long, loud blasts with forty men shouting, Wakey! Wakey! at the top of their voices. The next time we saw the couple, they said we had succeeded in waking them up, but the neighbours were complaining.

We moved to a camp at Caterham in Surrey and had to sleep rough in an old derelict house on the edge of the airfield. The previous night had been a heavy drinking session. Geordie Smith complained of feeling unwell, so we left him sleeping on the floor, as there were no beds. I had just driven away when a Doodlebug came down, exploding at the rear of the house. Turning my vehicle round and driving back, we ran into the building, expecting to find a dead Geordie. He was still fast asleep, snoring his head off. Waking him up he played holy hell with us for disturbing him. The force of the exploding flying-bomb had blown the back door off, shattering what few undamaged windows were left in the house, but Geordie had slept on undisturbed.

My time in this country was now running out, we six scruffy MT drivers were ordered back to Hatfield in Hertfordshire, to be replaced by other drivers. Some lucky devil was going to get the Studebaker. I had been with the gang for over five months and had driven them many miles. I had laughed with them; I had played hell with them; I had ignored them when trouble brewed and I had helped them when help was needed. I was now leaving for pastures unknown.

Having returned to Ashford, the two gangs gave us a farewell night to remember, beer flowed in the local and they were all gentlemen to the very end.

On arrival at Hatfield, we were informed we were overseas bound within the month. In the meantime we would be carrying out driving duties from Hatfield, delivering or fetching supplies in the South of England.

I set off early one evening for Portsmouth, a lousy, rainy night with a pea-souper of a fog. After making one call to collect some valuable equipment, I arrived at Rickmansworth. Seeing what appeared to be an empty market square, I decided to go no further and park up and sleep in the wagon.

Through the fog, I saw the eerie glow of a blue lamp shining on the wall of a police station. Recalling advice given to me during my driving course at Weeton, "If you ever need assistance, go to the police and if necessary make a bloody nuisance of yourselves, because if you ever return to civvy street, the police could be a nuisance to you." So in I went, requesting lodging for the night and a watch to be kept on the vehicle.

I was welcomed by the duty sergeant who appeared to be lonely. He left me in charge of the police station, going next door to the pub to fetch two pints of beer. We played cards and drank, had supper and then I was put in a cell with clean blankets and a promise he would not lock the cell door.

Asking me what time I wished to leave next morning, I said as early as possible. Waking me at nine o'clock, another sergeant apologised for not waking me earlier, explaining a dense fog still lingered outside and he thought I would like a lie-in. He placed a plate of bacon and eggs in front of me, which in those days were not to be objected to. I did not think for one moment I was taking any of his rations as he obviously had ways and means of obtaining food, which was in short supply. After breakfast, I was sent on my way with a genuine invitation to call again any time I was in the area.

Detailed to go into London one Saturday and on returning to Hatfield in the afternoon along Oxford Street, my wagon broke down. Even in wartime, the shops of London did not appear to lack customers. I must have created one of the biggest traffic jams Oxford Street had ever experienced.

Some days later the attack on Arnhem was launched and most of the massive glider force involved flew over the Hertfordshire area. One glider, having broken free from it's towing plane, crashed landed in a field on the edge of the village of Sandridge, near St. Albans. A guard was placed on the glider until it could be dismantled and taken away.

By the side of the field stood an old cottage, a middle-aged couple living there supplied the guards with tea. Transporting a guard to his duty, then fetching the other guard back, I also received a cup of tea from the couple. They invited me to visit them one weekend. Taking a mate with me, we slept on the stone hearth in front of a roaring fire. This couple were interesting country folk and I wrote to them from overseas, receiving letters in reply, but somehow the writing stopped.

One morning I went to nearby Hatfield House to deliver some documents. As I walked down the long drive, a Hillman Minx staff car drew up alongside me. The driver was an RAF officer. He asked me if I could direct him to the golf course and I sent him to the house. The officer was the legendary golfer, Henry Cotton, doing his bit by giving golfing exhibitions to RAF officers.

Stan Firmin, one of the six merry lads, invited three of us to his home in Luton for a weekend. His family gave us the time of our lives, we drank from Saturday lunchtime to Sunday night. The following weekend, Vicky Vickers, who came from Wembley, took the three of us to meet his family, a more sober family but they too made us very welcome.

Returning to camp on the Sunday night, the following morning I went home on seven days embarkation leave. This was my fourth leave in two and a half years, I could never understand how some chaps obtained a leave every three months.

I have not mentioned BRYLCREEM for a while. I still had not managed to get any and was still using bloody Anzora. I now had hopes of finally getting some BRYLCREEM in whichever part of the world I was heading for.

The leave turned out to be no different from my other leaves, just spent drinking. However, one amusing incident did occur. A pal, Walter, not in the forces through having a reserved occupation, was able to spend most nights with me. We were in that most palatial of all Sheffield establishments, the majestic Barley Corn in Cambridge Street.

On this night, as always, the place was full of American GI's and British servicemen. In true comradeship with our Allies, a fight broke out. Walter, eager to do his bit for King and Country let fly at an American with a stool, missed him and hit me. I saw stars – but no stripes and for the second time in my service life was dragged out of a pub just as things were getting exciting.

My leave over, I reported to West Kirby near Birkenhead, an overseas preparation camp, staying there for ten days. I was reunited with the other five lads who had been with me during the past six months – the six merry lads were together again.

We were formed into squads of fourteen men. A corporal was placed in charge of each squad from the time of our arrival to the day of our departure for overseas. These corporals were all well-known sportsmen, mostly footballers, who kitted-out airmen during the week and played football (not a bad life) at the weekends. Our corporal was a Scottish International footballer.

On the day of our departure we were assembled to be transported to Birkenhead railway station. Alongside the traditional 3-ton Bedford vehicle I was boarding was an RAF articulated lorry being loaded with our kit bags. The driver was my old school mate, Albert Marriott, whom I had last seen driving through Blackpool when we were on our initial MT driver training course. Albert and I were now in a position to talk and I was pleased to see a friendly face before setting off into the unknown.

Boarding the train at four o'clock on Friday afternoon, we assumed we were going across (or under) the Mersey to Liverpool to board a troopship. Five hours later, in the darkness of night, the train was still rattling along. As dawn broke we were travelling through the Scottish Highlands. At 11.30 am on a sunny Saturday morning we arrived at our destination, Port Glasgow, the train pulling up alongside the troopship, Tecleberg.

CHAPTER SEVEN

"WHERE ARE WE GOING?"
"SCHH... IT'S A SECRET"

We were hurried on to the troopship and it sailed at 12.30 p.m. We were on our way, or so we thought.

Sailing a few miles up the Clyde, the Tecleberg stopped. Right in the middle of the river off Gourock it dropped anchor, having missed a convoy. When the Tecleberg had dropped anchor that Saturday afternoon, no one was to know we would remain there for 14 days. Days and nights passed and new days dawned and we were still stranded there, with land to the left of us and land to the right of us.

The Tecleberg was a Polish vessel. Conditions on board were so bad that overnight chalked writing appeared over the decks, changing the name to the Altmark and that summed it up. (The Altmark had been a notorious German ship previously seized by the Royal Navy whilst transporting captured British servicemen from Norway to prisoner of war camps in Germany – the conditions on the Altmark had been inhuman.)

Sleeping accommodation down in the hold of the Tecleberg did not exist. The first night on board I attempted to climb into a hammock, fell out and did not make a second attempt, I slept on the floor fully dressed, stretched out head to toe along with everyone else. Food did not prevail, or would not have without potatoes, which were boiled in their jackets, the dirt from the fields where they had been collected still on them.

The one good thing on the ship was a small NAAFI shop. We could purchase as much chocolate and tinned fruit as we wanted and we lived on these items for over three weeks. The shop did not stock any BRYLCREEM but had boxes full of jars of bloody Anzora.

It was during the voyage I started to smoke – cigarettes were cheap and plentiful. Having no mugs, we drank 'sludged' tea out of empty fruit tins. We spent our time playing pontoon. To relieve the boredom in the evening I would wander to the stern of the ship and try to make conversation with an Indian crew member, who would be sitting working on an ancient Singer sewing machine, his bare feet pounding away on the treadle. On an upper deck, the officers lived a life of sheer luxury. We were not allowed up there, but we knew about it. As the officers gazed down from above with smiling faces, we looked up at them snarling and jeering. One of our mates, Don Taylor, had been a professional pianist in Civvy Street. In the evenings he was invited into the officers lounge to entertain them. He was wined and dined and when he related to us the meals being served up on that deck, he felt embarrassed. We told Don to enjoy them.

Waking up to the throb of the ship's engines, on the fifteenth morning after leaving Port Glasgow, we scampered up onto the deck to find the ship was finally moving. Five troopships sailing in a single file escorted by a large naval force. We had been watching the escort for only a short while when the leading troopship and a number of escort vessels were seen to veer to the right, then sail in a circle. We thought, "Christ, we are going back." Seeing Belfast in the distance, another troopship steamed out to join us. At last, we were definitely on our way.

There is not a lot I wish to say about the journey, there is not a lot I wish to remember. On board were 2,500 servicemen, of which 1,500 were members of the Free French Army. On departure from Port Glasgow we had been informed our destination was a military secret, even the ship's crew said they did not know where we were heading. The Frenchmen knew and told us – Algiers. Obviously the French did not believe in military secrets.

Entertainment on board had to be arranged amongst ourselves. The French chaps decided to organise a boxing match, inviting anyone to fight one of their fellows. A squad of Scottish soldiers put forward one of their mates, claiming he was the Regimental Champion. We did not know the lad but, with the opposition being 'froggies', he had our support. The contestants entered the makeshift ring, formed by a circle of men crowding round the deck, shook hands and the fight began. There were just two hits in the contest, the Frenchman hit the Scot, who hit the deck – the fight was over. With gentlemanly apologies from the Frenchmen, there were a lot of red, white and blue faces amongst the British contingent.

As the Tecleberg sailed on and into the Mediterranean Sea, a member of it's crew, a Lascar seaman died, (he possibly thought it was the only way he could get off the ship). The following day we assembled to witness a simple, but moving burial service conducted by an Army Padre. With the engines of the ship closed down, there was an air of complete silence as the sack, containing the seaman's body, was tipped overboard and splashed into the ocean. It was an unforgettable experience.

We sailed into Sicily, but didn't disembark. The Sicilians did not appear to want us, for within two hours of arriving we steamed away. One of the escorting warships, a destroyer, then livened up the journey by dropping depth charges. I did not see any U-boats come to the surface, only plenty of dead fish. The ship's cook should have picked them up to go with his potatoes, we could have had fish and chips.

Eventually, zig-zagging past rusting hulks of partly submerged ships, the Tecleberg sailed into the North African port of Algiers. We were taken, not by an expected 3-ton Bedford, but by a 3-ton Chevrolet to a transit camp, round the other side of Algiers bay. Being 'wanderers', we were to remain there until a good home could be found for us, but not in Algiers.

The MT section of the camp was short of drivers and placed the welcome mat out for we six merry lads. Supplied with a 3-ton Chevrolet wagon, I spent six weeks transporting departing airmen to and collecting new arrivals from the port of Algiers.

The evenings were spent drinking in a small Arab bar located in a village one mile from the camp. To get to the bar, we had to walk past a row of luxurious bungalows situated on a beach. These bungalows were owned by wealthy French businessmen.

Destroyer escort of our convoy, 1943.

Night after night we downed bottles of Muscatel wine, which could be drunk all night without any apparent effect, until we walked outside into the fresh air, then the alcohol really struck you. The Algerian Arabs were not the friendliest of people. It was only by walking back to camp in a crowd that we were safe from being attacked.

We had been issued with meppachrine (quinine) tablets as a protection against malaria. One evening with the Muscatel flowing, one of the lads put a meppachrine tablet in 'Shorty' Long's drink. Taking a swig from his glass, the poor devil almost choked. Rushing to the bar and complaining, Shorty made the Arab owner of the bar, Abdhulla, drink out of the glass. Abdhulla almost choked. We were sat at the back of the room almost hysterical with laughter, Shorty and Abdhulla far from amused. I thought, "Oh Christ, another fight, in another bar," but not this time on the peaceful dockside of Aberdeen, or in the majestic Barley Corn in Sheffield, but on foreign territory. Abdhulla, realising the large amounts of money we spent each night, supplied Shorty with another drink. Although the atmosphere cooled down, the other Arab customers kept their eyes firmly fixed on our table.

The camp was surrounded by extensive orange groves, guarded by a lone Arab. A couple of the lads would make for one end of the grove, the Arab following them, making sure he had his beady eyes on them. We would enter the grove from the other end, returning with our arms full of oranges.

Accommodated in tents, we were advised to sleep in our clothes and to keep our boots on, as the Arabs would creep in and steal them, – they must have been trained in the hostels of Aberdeen or Manchester. No one advised us how to protect the tents, the Arabs were experts at stealing them while you

NO BRYLCREEM - NO MEDALS

slept. I had visions of waking up in the morning looking at blue skies, fortunately I never did.

Driving into the port of Algiers one morning, I witnessed an impressive and unforgettable scene. A number of dead German soldiers were being carried off an hospital ship on stretchers, draped with Swastika's and placed onto motor launches. They were then brought ashore to where I stood on the quayside. Two British soldiers with heads bowed presented arms in a salute of respect to the dead Germans. It was a moving tribute. The relatives of those dead Germans would never know of that solemn ceremony.

The hospital ship was Italian and having been encountered by the Royal Navy out in the Mediterranean Sea was listing dangerously. When the Italian ship's Captain was asked by the Royal Naval Commander if they required assistance, he replied, "No!" A number of British sailors were then ordered to board the hospital ship. The boarding party discovered the ship to be full of badly wounded German military personnel, but also carrying large amounts of arms and ammunition. The Royal Navy escorted the ship into Algiers, docking it between two landing stages to prevent anyone escaping.

One afternoon, twenty of us went into the Kasbah, the market quarter of Algiers. In this district there was always safety in large numbers. All members of the British armed forces had, by a military order, to be out of the area by six o'clock in the evening, the Kasbah then being declared out of bounds. While walking through a narrow alley, a young girl approached us, offering herself. One of the lads in our party, whom I did not know well, said he was going with her. We warned him not to go, but he still went. He was never seen again by us. Later, we were informed what had happened to him – arguing with the girl over her price, she fetched two Arabs who kept him locked in a room. At curfew time the Arabs went and fetched the military police, who regularly patrolled the area. When they arrived at the room and opened the door, the airman, thinking it was the Arabs returning, pulled out a knife. He was arrested and had not returned to camp when we finally moved out seven days later.

Our day of departure from Algiers came. Taken to the port, we boarded the troopship Champollian, a French owned ex-passenger liner. Life and conditions on this ship were to be a lot different to those we had experienced on the Tecleberg. Apart from 20 RAF personnel, there were 1,000 African soldiers on board. Once again, as when we had left Port Glasgow, our destination was a military secret. The Africans knew and as with the French who had told us we were going to Algiers, they informed us we were heading for Alexandria in Egypt. Their Secret Service was either inefficient or, like the French, they did not have one.

During the journey we were given the best of jobs connected with the galley, carrying sides of beef from the refrigerators below in the hold and up two flights of steep steps to the galley. Although the work was heavy, it was enjoyable. We were supplied with as much food as we could eat, which was ideal until the ship sailed, then our stomachs rebelled.

The only complaint I had of the Champollian was that there was not any BRYLCREEM on board. Like the Americans at Ramsbury back in the UK, the French thought it was cream to put in coffee.

Following our arrival at the port of Alexandria, in Egypt, we were transported to a transit camp at Heliopolis on the outskirts of Cairo, where we stayed for two days. Then came

NO BRYLCREEM - NO MEDALS

the break up of we six merry lads, after having been together for over eight months – three went to one camp, two to another and I, all alone again, climbed aboard a train to Suez.

The Egyptian railways had to be travelled on to be believed. I had to fight my way on to the train, then fight for a seat, put my kit bag on the seat and sit on it. There were more non fare-paying passengers than paying ones. Arabs were hanging onto the sides of the carriages or running along the roofs. A one legged Arab in a black galabiya which had once been white, a battered red fez perched on his grey curly hair, sprinted along the roof supported by a piece of wood used as a crutch.

I joined a squad of bush-hatted Australian soldiers who gave me a journey of good cheer, beer flowing like the River Nile, but cleaner. Vendors walked up and down the carriages selling everything from coffee in big filthy urns strapped to their backs, to trash souvenirs and dirty postcards, but no BRYLCREEM. Three prostitutes paraded their wares, (where on the train they provided their services was a mystery). Two of the Aussies were tempted, but their mates dissuaded them. Arriving at Suez, a port of dirt and smells and heat, half drunk, I waved my farewell to the Aussies and climbed on to an inevitable waiting 3-ton Bedford wagon and was transported to Shallufa.

CHAPTER EIGHT

"BLOODY THIS AND BLOODY THAT!"

AF Shallufa was a camp training aircrews on Baltimore medium bomber aircraft. All flying personnel, including the Commanding Officer, were South Africans, of whom I came to have a lot of respect.

So much was to happen in so short a space of time; light-hearted moments, of which there were many, and tragedies of which there were too many. I could never have visualised on that first day as I went through the main gates of Shallufa that within twelve months I would be in hospital fighting for my life, then recovering from an illness that could have taken it, as it did to five of my friends and another 19 lads from the camp. During the previous two and a half years I had my various 'ups and downs', and I later realised that it was during those twelve months at Shallufa that I grew up.

So to the first night at RAF Shallufa. After meeting my new mates of the scruffy MT section, (and we got scruffier) and having sobered up from my train journey, it was into the NAAFI. Looking round the crowded room, I made my now familiar, optimistic, hushed request for a jar of BRYLCREEM. The chap behind the counter had a wonderful sense of humour. He told me in an equally hushed voice, "Come back after the war is over, mate." then, "Here's a jar of bloody Anzora, free. We can't sell the bloody stuff. In fact we can't even give the

NO BRYLCREEM - NO MEDALS

chuffing stuff away!" – I now considered having all my hair shaved off.

The fun started the following day, on my first drive on Egyptian roads. I was detailed to take a corporal to the 13th General Army Hospital near Suez, I was to spend a long time in that hospital later. Driving out of the camp and turning right, I was on my way. It was a straight sandy dirt-track road. I noticed a lorry, an Arab gharry, approaching me on the same side of the road. Still dreaming of driving along peaceful English country lanes, I did not realise that I was on the wrong side and the approaching wagon was on his correct side. Considering that I had experienced no problems while driving on the right hand side of the road in Algiers, the sun must have got at me already.

As we got closer to the gharry, the corporal sitting at my side timed his remarks to perfection, "If you don't bloody well shift to the other bloody side of the bloody road, he bloody well won't, and then we'll get a more comfortable bloody ride

An RAF Baltimore.

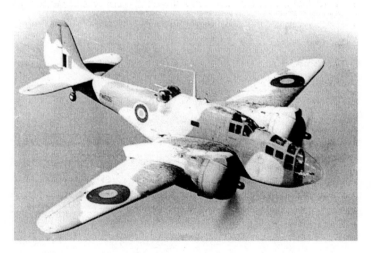

to where we are bloody well going!" – That is a mild printable interpretation of his actual words – I did shift! Having no further trouble during the rest of the journey, we arrived at the entrance to the hospital, straight through the gates and reaching a roundabout, I drove round it the wrong way. My passenger turned out to be a very brave man, he actually came back to camp with me, I had learned my lesson.

I soon settled down to camp life. There was a sergeant, corporal, ten drivers and three mechanics in the MT section, we were a happy crowd. There were different types of vehicles, all in no better condition than the ones in Britain. Duties varied, some interesting, some boring. Shallufa had the living quarters, MT section, Cookhouse, Sick-bay and NAAFI surrounded by a high barbed wire fence. The control tower and runways, perimeters and storage bays for the aircraft were outside. Two miles out into the desert were the bomb and ammunition dumps. It was while returning from these dumps, the amusing episode of getting lost in the desert took place.

A troop of East African soldiers were stationed on the camp, their duties were to guard these dumps 24 hours a day in two shifts of 12 hours, four men to a shift. Their corporal spoke only eight words of English, which included bloody this and bloody that, being repeated every second word. Although he did not understand their meanings, he was proud of his knowledge. The other members of the troop, not only could not speak English, they could not speak the language of their own country. An Australian soldier who had lived and worked in East Africa had been brought in specifically to teach them to speak their native tongue.

The MT section supplied a vehicle to transport these men out and back again to the dumps, the driver on a rota basis.

The corporal went along with the driver each time to supervise the change over of guards, sitting in the front of the wagon making good conversation, bloody this and bloody that, which took up most of his vocabulary, his other words were "God Save the King" – but which king? Probably some ruler in a mud hut in the jungle!

To reach these dumps we drove out of the camp passing the flying area and on to a sand-track, we were dependant on lumps of rock for guidance. In the daytime it was not a problem, but in the darkness of night it became a different matter. As I approached the dump, a guard would stand in the middle of the track, his rifle pointed towards the windscreen and my head. I would stop. No one had ever dared to ignore him, the corporal would get out and identify himself, only then were we allowed to proceed. I have never seen a squad of men so dedicated to their duties. It was a known fact that if any of these men did anything wrong, their punishment was to be taken off guard duty. They were a proud race.

Going out at night in the dark, looking for those lumps of rock at the side of the track with only the beam of my headlights to pick them out, I then had to judge the guard's position. Suddenly, and almost upon him, my headlights would pick him out, standing erect in the middle of the track. His black face almost obscured, but his white teeth flashing, his rifle pointed at my head. Never once during the night-run, which I did a number of times, did it fail to make my hair stand on end, 'Anzora' and all. That also went for my mates.

Having arrived at these dumps one night, the guards had been changed and we were returning to camp. Somehow I missed a lump of rock and when I should have been seeing the lights of the camp in the distance – nothing! I kept driving, with no track or lumps of rock to guide me. The corporal jabbering away with his eight-word vocabulary, the bumping and rocking of the vehicle had the poor devils in the back hitting the canvas roof and then the floor. Suddenly, I saw lights in the far distance, but too many to be the camp. Keeping going, the lights gradually coming nearer, I reached a road which I recognised as the Shallufa to Suez road, the lights of Suez still a good distance away. I then drove the three miles to the camp, entering through the main gate.

The SP's on duty scratched their heads, the corporal and his men having enjoyed every minute of it. Back in the billet, my mates considered it a great achievement to go out by the top gate and return in through the main gate, old Hamby had done a first. It took a lot of living down. The following night, as I was setting off, one of the lads stood in front of my wagon with a red lamp, volunteering to guide me there and back. I later did that trip a number of times at night, never managing to find that other road back, much to the disappointment of the corporal and his men.

Once a week the duty officer had to be taken out to the ammunition dumps. On one occasion I took the catering officer, the most unpopular officer on the camp – I will mention him again later. Going in daylight with the corporal sitting in the rear of the wagon, the officer sat at my side, we approached the dump. The guard stood in the middle of the track, his rifle pointing towards my head commanding me to stop. I stopped. The officer ordered me to proceed, I refused. I knew the penalty for disobeying an officer and I was prepared to face any Court Martial. I reported the incident to the MT sergeant, who agreeing with me, regretted the officer never took any action against me.

Outside the camp's main gate was a row of thirty tattered tents, they were filthy, repulsive and stunk – better described as hovels – where the Arabs who carried out all menial tasks on the camp existed. These people would bow to you in the daytime, but stab you in the back at night.

One Arab worker, Hafid, whom I would never class with the other Arabs, is worth recalling. Prior to my arrival at Shallufa, a Beaufighter fighter-bomber landed and while taxiing round the perimeter a section of it's undercarriage collapsed. The plane veered to it's left, ploughing into the duty crash tender and killing two of the vehicle's crew. Hafid, who was working nearby, ran to the tender and dragged the corporal in charge clear of the plane's propellers. In recognition of his action, Hafid was given a rise of one 'Acker' a day, which to him was a lot of money and he was placed in charge of all the

The Author, Shallufa, 1944.

other Arab workers. He became devoted to the corporal whose life he had saved.

Hafid lived in a village by the side of the Sweetwater canal. If ever there was a misnomer, that was one. One Saturday, Hafid's sister was getting married and the MT personnel together with his corporal 'mate' were invited to the reception. We debated whether to go, Hafid guaranteed our safety. Normally on Saturday nights a liberty truck went to Suez, but on this occasion we used it to go to the reception, which turned out to be a riotous feast. The bride and groom got drunk, the villagers and our lot got drunk, the camels and even the oxen monotonously ambling around the well pulling up water got drunk. On what we never knew. I was not driving that night.

An incident occurred a week after the wedding making me suspicious about the friendliness of those Arabs who had been our hosts at the wedding. I was detailed to take an officer to Suez one night. I drove out of camp in pitch darkness and on to an unlit track, dependant on my vehicle's headlights to guide me. The skies were cloudless, the colour a deep blue-black. Almost every star in the universe could be seen, appearing to be looking down on you.

The officer had only just remarked, "It looks like we are driving on another planet," when I spotted a white-sheeted figure standing in the middle of the road. Having been warned there had been previous attempts at ambushing, I told the officer I feared this could be one. I increased my speed. At the last minute the Arab attempted to move away from the vehicle, but I struck him. The officer said he had seen another group of Arabs waiting some yards away. My heart was beating faster than the pistons of the engine, as I prayed they would keep going – they did!

Arriving in Suez, I drove to an Army camp, reported the incident and given a military escort back to camp. Passing the spot where the attempted ambush had occurred, it was deserted. That incident happened within one mile from the village where we had gone to the wedding. Hafid never mentioned it, but if that Arab I hit lived, he would have been crippled for life.

Apart from the hair-raising happenings, there were amusing ones. Most Sunday mornings, the local Arabs brought their asses or mules to compete in donkey races. It was not exactly Epsom or Ascot, but it brought a touch of the Sport of Kings to Egypt. The event was classed as the Shallufa Derby. The main problem was that week after week the same ass, 'Cairo Jack', won. One of our MT mates, 'Bookie' Bailey was the camp bookmaker. We decided something had to be done to help him re-coup his losses.

3 RAF pals, Shallufa, 1944.

Before the start of the race a dish of water would be placed on the ground for each animal. On this notable Sunday morning, when filling the dishes with water, we filled Cairo Jack's with whisky. He took one sip, liked it and drank the lot.

Under starter's orders, then they were away, with Cairo Jack getting off to his usual flying start. Approaching the course's equivalence to Epsom's Tattenham Corner he swerved, colliding with the runners to his right, then careered into the runners to his left. Riders were falling like rows of skittles, red Fezzes were flying through the air, their galabiya's wrapped around their necks. Cairo Jack then finished his spectacle off by turning a complete circle, heading for the camp gates and scattering all the spectators in his path. His unseated rider lay floundering on the ground, praying and wailing to Allah and all the other gods he could think of. In the meantime, the 'Suez Flyer', which every week always finished last, had managed to avoid the fallen runners and won. No one had backed it.

That night in the NAAFI we celebrated a great victory, all drinks on Bookie Bailey. It was the only time I had witnessed 'ass nobbling'. Cairo Jack was never brought back to compete in the races and no other ass took it's place as favourite.

Shallufa was a good camp for home-made entertainment. Apart from the donkey races, we also had cockroach races, the 'Shallufa Cockroach Handicap'. Held at meal times, it created much enthusiasm amongst the diners. The racecourse was in the comfort of the cook-house, where rivers of steam cascaded down it's walls. A paradise where the large, black, fat beetles thrived, crawling along to their hearts content, the cooks tickling their rear ends with stew-serving ladles. The cockroaches that did not fall into the cauldrons of corned beef stew stood a good chance of winning.

Bookie Bailey, never one to miss the opportunity to make money, gave generous odds on the races. Knowing there were many 'fallers', he was on to a good thing. Bookie would even take bets on which lad would be served with a stewed cockroach on his plate!

From the outside, the camp cinema was a large, unsightly concrete building. Inside, wooden chairs were placed in mass disarray. One afternoon the film 'Laura' was being shown to a packed audience, the Egyptian heat drifting from the outside and into the dark, airless room, where everyone was stripped to the waist with sweat streaming down their bodies.

All eyes were transfixed on to the screen where, with the haunting theme music in the background, the male star of the film, Dana Andrews, was taking Laura into his arms, and about to give her, her first kiss.

Suddenly a lone voice shouted "RATS!" The room having been invaded by an army of large rats, some as big as rabbits. Uproar and turmoil then reigned in the darkened cinema, with chairs flying all over the place as they were smashed on to the floor or over the heads of several unfortunate lads.

Eventually, having got rid of the rats that had survived the onslaught, normality and peace returned, then groans of discontentment from the audience when they realised that Laura, having received and enjoyed her first kiss, had departed from the screen.

During the day a silver coloured Avro Anson flew regularly over the camp, a gift from the British Government to it's pilot, King Farouk. We would raise our eyes to the sky chanting the ditty of King Farouk hanging his "B...ks" on a hook, not forgetting to mention Queen Farida.

CHRISTMAS DINNER
RAF SHALLUFA 1944   AIRMENS' MESS

CREAM of CHICKEN SOUP
ROAST TURKEY & ROAST PORK — SAVOURY STUFFING
GRAVY ~ APPLE & BREAD SAUCES ~ ROAST & CREAMED
POTATOES ~ MACÉDOINE & FRESH GREEN VEGETABLES
CHRISTMAS PUDDING & BRANDY SAUCE ~ MINCE PIES-JELLIES
CHEESE ~ DESSERT & MIXED NUTS ~ BEER ~ CIGARETTES
MINERALS

Christmas 1944 at RAF Shallufa. Missed by the author due to imbibing 'spiked' beer on Xmas eve!

Christmas 1944 arrived and a party was held in the billet, a bar fixed in a corner. I started drinking at six o'clock on Christmas Eve night, by nine o'clock I was out like a light. A mechanic, 'Sparky' Spencer, who claimed to be a pal of mine, had laced my beer with gin. I awoke at six o'clock Christmas Day night having missed my Christmas dinner, but they did present me with a copy of the menu. Very little to say about that Christmas!

One of our duties was driving the petrol bowser. These vehicles held 950 gallons of high-octane aircraft fuel. Prior to being stored in a parking bay, all aircraft had to be re-fuelled at the close of each day's flying. The small donkey engine operating the bowser had to be cranked before fuel could be pumped out of the tank.

Standing at the side of the bowser one evening waiting for a Baltimore aircraft to arrive, a guard walked over to talk to me and asked for a cigarette. He dropped his loaded rifle, which fired when it hit the ground, the bullet missed him and me and 950 gallons of fuel, speeding off into the desert.

The Commanding Officer, a South African, was a popular and well-respected fellow with all ranks. He regularly flew an old Wellington bomber, – this aircraft was literally tied together with string, he thought the world of it – to meet a friend in Cairo. A fitter and I would wait for his return to re-fuel the plane. When he eventually arrived back at camp the CO was always most apologetic for having kept us waiting, explaining to us of non-existent head winds having slowed him down. He would then give us 'ten bob' each, or the equivalent in Ackers.

An amusing incident involving this CO occurred, although for once he was not amused. He possessed a dog, 'Sandy', a damned nuisance that barked incessantly. One evening as dusk was falling, Sandy was on the inside of the protective fencing barking his head off. A pyard, a wild desert dog, – these animals could be heard howling throughout the night out in the desert – came up to the other side of the fence barking at Sandy. A patrolling guard, fed up with the hullabaloo going on, fired his rifle at the pyard, missed and killed Sandy. During Sandy's demise, a mournful tune could be heard in the background being played on a violin by the Medical Officer, helped along by the generous helpings of scotch whisky he was very fond of. We suggested to the CO that Sandy be honoured with a military funeral.

Regular trips were made to Suez for supplies. On the return journey, as we approached a railway crossing, an Arab boy waited, holding baskets of tangerines and bananas for sale. Slowing down the wagon, my passenger would lean out of the cab, then grabbing a handful of fruit would push the basket and the boy to the ground. I would then release the clutch and race away, the Arab boy disputing our parentage shouting, "You white bastards!" If there was one thing plentiful in Egypt, apart from filth and sand, it was fruit.

Nights off-duty were spent in the billet writing or reading letters to and from home, studying the anatomy of Betty Grable or playing pontoon, the stakes for the games being cigarettes, which were cheap and plentiful. By the end of the night, with the cigarettes having constantly changed hands, the tobacco had vanished leaving only cigarette paper.

I received regular parcels of 'The News of the World' newspaper from my Grandmother. These were popular amongst all my mates, who devoured every inch of the scandal stories and sports pages. It was the only time peace and quiet existed in the billet.

 Bob 'Rommel' Smith, was of small build. At night, when the temperature dropped and it did in winter, if Bob had a duty run, he would go out wearing his drivers peaked cap and a great-coat reaching down to his ankles, hence the nickname Rommel. Bob and I spent many hours in conversation. Coming from a poor family in Blackburn, he spoke of going out into the streets to steal food for the family to live on. Bob did not boast, he was truthful. He had been a boxer in Civvy Street.

One evening, with a lot of fooling around going on in the billet, 'Lofty' Evans, a tall, lanky lad, another humorous character as well as a practical joker, put his hands up inviting

NO BRYLCREEM - NO MEDALS

Bob to hit him. Bob took Lofty at his word and hit him. Lofty went down like a log, it was a pure accident and Bob was distraught. When Lofty had recovered, he and Bob embraced each other, but Bob was never challenged again.

Shower time at Shallufa was an event of great amusement and ingenuity. The shower was a tall iron frame embedded in the ground, an empty oil drum perched on the top. While I stood underneath, having rubbed my feet in a tray of powder to prevent foot rot, a pal climbed a rickety ladder and poured dirty, rusty water into the drum, the water spraying out unevenly through holes punched in the bottom, giving me a thorough soaking. The operation would then be reversed, with myself still wet through, climbing the ladder and giving him the same treatment.

One of the few impressive sights at Shallufa was to look out across the flat desert land towards the Suez Canal and see warships, especially aircraft carriers, moving along. It was hard to believe these great ships were floating on water.

My 21st birthday came and went, I attached no great importance to the occasion. That day I drove a wagon to Cairo for supplies, being accompanied by a trainee driver, 'Jock' Douglas. After loading my wagon we had a couple of drinks, then visited the Pyramids. We attempted to ride a camel but fell off, then decided to return to camp.

CHAPTER NINE

DEATHS IN THE DESERT

O n RAF aerodromes, while flying is in operation, a crash ambulance (blood wagon) and the crash tender are positioned at the side of the control tower. The drivers of both these vehicles were from the MT section and normally volunteers. The drivers at the time were requesting to return to normal duties, two replacements being required. The ambulance driver told me to have a 'bash' at it, claiming it was a cushy job, receiving better food than the stuff dished out in the cook-house – without cockroaches – and being billeted in the sick bay, sleeping in a more comfortable bed. Up to this time there had been no plane crashes. I decided to take the job, accompanied by my mate Tommy Sampson who would drive the crash tender.

These duties involved two shifts, morning and afternoon. Most of the flying was by crews training on 'circuits and bumps'. We spent the duty watching the planes take off, fly around the aerodrome, land, taxi round the perimeter and take off again, not very exciting stuff.

Before going on duty we went to the NAAFI, bought bottles of pop and packets of nuts then drove to the control tower. With our pop and nuts we would sit on the bonnets of our vehicles. One of the crash tender's crew had a ukulele and with a song-book we had a sing-song. What could be better?

NO BRYLCREEM - NO MEDALS

The ambulance was an old, ancient Albion – another relic from World War One – and very temperamental to start. To get it started I had to crank the engine with a starting handle. This engine had a nasty habit of kick-back and was liable to break a wrist if you did not get out of the way quickly enough. It's maximum speed was between 25 and 30 mph. For the vital duty it had to fulfil, this ambulance was a disgrace.

The medical orderly who shared the duty with me was a likeable, humorous character, 'Sid', a cockney. Sid's claim to fame before joining the RAF was having played as a trumpeter in Nat Gonella's band. Sid never took part in our sing-songs, he would spend the entire duty sleeping on a stretcher in the back of the ambulance. Sid and I got on famously, when he was awake.

The corporal in charge of the crash tender, 'Windy' Woodall, was a neurotic type who should never have been on this duty, let alone in charge of it. Windy would stand well in front of the vehicles, watching every plane as it landed, follow it's progress to the end of the runway, until it turned and taxied round the perimeter, then proceeded to the runway for the next take off. From our position, after the plane had touched down and taxied along the runway, we eventually lost sight of it because of the position of the control tower. I could never understand why we were never in line with the control tower.

One evening duty, with pop and nuts being devoured and a sing-song well under way, Sid was as usual in the back of the ambulance snoring his head off. Windy suddenly shouted, "A plane has overshot the runway and crashed into the sand." I started the ambulance, Tommy started the crash tender and we raced down the perimeter at full throttle, side by side. We suddenly saw the Baltimore looming towards us, the pilot must have got the shock of his life, seeing us bearing down on him. He turned his landing headlights on. In a perfect formation, I veered to the right, Tommy to the left and we raced back to our standpoint with the plane chasing us.

In the meantime, Sid, having been asleep in the back, had fallen off his stretcher and in trying to climb through a small window into the cab, had got stuck and was yelling his head off. I had one hand on the steering wheel, my other hand trying to free Sid, the ambulance swaying and careering all over the perimeter, being chased by a Baltimore aircraft.

Arriving back at the stand-point, together with the crash tender crew minus Windy Woodall – we had put him in Coventry, no one was speaking to him – we struggled to free Sid. Having just released him, the pilot of the plane who had completed his last circuit and bumps for the day came up to us. With a wide grin on his face and with a strong South African dialect, he said, "That put the screaming sh...s up you!" It may have appeared funny to him and amusing to us, but it could have turned out nasty for Sid, giving him a bad injury. I told him he could have been invalided back home wounded in the course of duty, "Stuck in the back of an ambulance!" The one who really got our wrath was Windy Woodall, unfortunately it did not stop him panicking during future duties.

Life carried on normally, until a period of 36 hours, which has lived vividly in my memory to this day. During a morning flight, one of Shallufa's Baltimore aircraft crashed into Suez Bay. A number of aircraft had previously crashed into this bay, one theory put forward for this was air pockets, but never proved.

Although I had been on duty the previous night and was now on a rest period, I was detailed to take our violin-playing

MO to Suez. Arriving, an air-sea rescue launch and crew were waiting to take us out into the Bay. The launch crew had already spent a considerable time searching, without finding any wreckage, a buoy had been placed over the spot where the plane had presumably crashed. When we arrived at the scene a blood-stained parachute had floated to the surface, but no bodies or debris could be found. I picked the parachute up, returned with it to camp, handing it to the CO who, after examination gave it back to me with instructions to take it outside the camp area and burn it. I was back on duty in the afternoon.

As well as circuits and bumps training, five aircraft would take off on an advanced training flight. They first flew long distance on a navigational exercise. On their return to Shallufa they flew over the camp, then proceeded to a bombing range in the desert for the bomb-aimer to release bombs on to a target. The aircraft returned, flying close to the camp for gunnery practice. We would watch tracer bullets being fired by the front gunner raining down into a target.

During one of these flights, four planes had already returned, gone through their bombing and gunnery exercises, landed and completed their flying for the day. We sat by our vehicles waiting for the fifth plane to return. The duty normally finished at ten o'clock. At two o'clock in the morning, we were still waiting. The control tower eventually advised us to go off duty.

At eight o'clock later that morning I was fetched out of bed and told the missing plane had blown up in the desert about twenty miles from Shallufa, I was detailed to take a vehicle with medical personnel and equipment. Reaching a certain point, a group of Arabs guided us on trackless, stony ground to the scene of the crash. The debris of the plane was scattered over a wide area. Our task should have been to rescue the crew or survivors, we now had to find their remains. Two bodies, amazingly, were intact, the other two bodies we picked up bit by bit and placed into bags. I drove back to camp in a daze. Eight young airmen had died within twelve hours.

Back on duty at four o'clock in the afternoon, neither my mates or I had any heart for a sing-song. We did not even drink pop or eat nuts. We sat silently, watching the pilots doing their monotonous circuits and bumps. The aircraft on the advanced training flights started to return. The third aircraft flew over the camp, proceeded to the bombing range, returned for the gunnery practice and with the gunner firing into his target, the Baltimore dived into the ground bursting into flames.

Arriving at the scene, the heat was too intense for us to get near the aircraft. It was a hopeless situation. Eventually, having extinguished the fire and recovered the charred bodies – the smell of burning flesh never leaves one – we returned with our gruesome burden to the camp. The toll of airmen who had lost their lives in 36 hours was now twelve.

Going into the dining room, a large meal had been placed on the table. I sat staring at it. Sid said, "Eat it up, Hamby." I moved the food away and got up, went outside and was violently sick! Music from a wireless set drifted out from an open window – Glenn Miller's recording of 'The Story of a Starry Night.' I looked up into an inky-black, starry night sky. The pyards out beyond the camp fences were howling.

I returned into the dining room, where Sid had finished his meal and was eating mine. With the thoughts of the crash still pounding in my head, the scene was still vivid and clear, especially the charred bodies of the crew. I then realised that when we were at the blazing aircraft, ammunition had been exploding in all directions. As I sat down, Sid put his hand on my shoulder saying, "You did OK, Hamby."

The following morning I had no rest. I had the grim task of transferring the bodies of the crew from our sick-bay to the military hospital mortuary near Suez. On arrival at the mortuary, a solemn act of respect to the men was carried out by the attendant and I. We draped the Union Jack over each body, then carried the stretcher into the mortuary.

My thoughts had already gone out to the relatives of those men and the other eight men, all South Africans, who had died within the last 36 hours, realising that they had yet to be informed of their tragic loss. Two days later, I drove a vehicle carrying colleagues of the dead airmen to the burials at a military cemetery.

On my return to camp from the mortuary, I had gone to see 'Tubby' Walker, the MT corporal, requesting I resume normal duties. Tubby was happy about my request, suggesting I work with him in his office on the clerical side of the section. I was now back with my mates. This duty was unfortunately to last only four weeks.

After Tubby had left the office one morning saying that he would be away for only a short time, the Armoury Officer walked in requesting a vehicle and driver to transport him to the bombing range. With no other drivers being available, I left a note on the desk telling Tubby where I had gone. I went and collected a 15 cwt Chevrolet. The officer got in and as I was driving away, Tubby walked up to the vehicle asking me where I was going, I told him, the officer confirming it. Tubby said he needed the drive, took my place and drove away. Finishing work at four o'clock, I went back to the billet and fell asleep. I awoke at six o'clock just as the MT sergeant and

'Drummy' Drummond, a driver walked in. Both were distressed, their faces chalk white. The sergeant said, "There's been an accident, Tubbys dead."

To a silent room, he explained that the Armoury Officer and another officer had arranged to go out that evening. When the Armoury Officer had not returned to the officers mess for his meal, his friend contacted the MT sergeant and it was realised Tubby's wagon had not returned. Thinking that Tubby had broken down, he set off with Drummy to find them.

The sergeant continued, "When we found the Chevrolet out in the desert it appeared to be parked with no sign of it's occupants, I sensed there was something more serious than a breakdown. We had an eerie feeling something sinister had happened. Drummy and I walked to the vehicle and stood looking around. A short distance away we noticed the ground appeared to have been disturbed. Walking to the spot we looked down into a crater and saw the remains of the officer and Tubby, both had walked onto an unexploded bomb. They had been blown in half."

Collecting medical personnel we returned to search, I drove one vehicle, Drummy the other. As it had now gone dark, an Avro Anson aircraft flew above us dropping flares. We searched for over two hours without finding either the Chevrolet or the bodies of the officer and Tubby. Our main concern was the pyard dogs that roamed the desert at night, they could find the bodies and eat them. At a time like this, one realises what a desolate and forbidding area the desert is. A wagon was driven out at dawn, going straight to the spot, returning with it's gruesome contents. I thanked God I had been spared that task.

The following day the MT sergeant came to me, "I'm not ordering you Hamby, but asking you if you will drive the wagon which will be bearing Tubby's coffin to his burial?" He knew I was distressed, but thought it correct to ask. I agreed. It was hard to believe that I was going to drive the vehicle Tubby would have been driving to my funeral!

The burial took place at a remote, small, sandy cemetery for both the officer and Tubby. There was no disparity in rank. When a lone bugler blew the Last Post and the Guard of Honour fired their rifles into the air, I bowed my head and thought, "But for thirty seconds, the coffin being lowered into the ground could have been mine!" I have had many thoughts over the years and always will, of that lonely grave out there in the Egyptian sands.

Returning to camp from the funeral, the MT sergeant and I went into the MT office. As he was removing Tubby's tool box, he said, "Take something, Hamby." I took a small tyre pressure gauge, which I still have today. He told me if I wanted Tubby's job, I could have it. He would arrange for me to be made up to corporal, I declined.

I came off office duties and returned to driving. So much had happened in so short a space of time. I was smoking and drinking heavily. I had a feeling of depression that I would never return home, although I could not imagine what else could happen to me. Something did, and in a way I never expected.

News came into the camp one night from Europe – Berlin, the capital of Germany had fallen. The NAAFI at a small RAF Transit Camp ten miles distant from Shallufa had a surplus of beer. They decided to have a Berlin Night in the hope of getting rid of it, letting it be known amongst other Suez Canal Zone RAF camps. I was on duty that night when a message was received at midnight, stating that two airmen from our camp were stranded there. (I had no idea how the hell they had got there, but they had). The camp was requesting a wagon be sent to collect the men, for their own safety. I was far from happy at having to turn out and drive ten miles at that time of the night (this was regarding my own safety). A mate, not on duty, went with me. That consideration highlighted the wonderful comradeship existing at Shallufa.

What the people at the camp requesting me to go did not say was that the two men I had to collect had been involved in a fight and one was hurt. Not only had they been in a fight, but had fought each other. A Scotsman and a Cockney, both bosom pals. They were so drunk that the Cockney had smashed a glass and pushed it into his pal's face. When I arrived, they were comforting each other, the Scots lad's face a bloody mess. They drunkenly apologised to me for having to turn out so late. Bundling them both into the back of the wagon, we returned to camp, knowing that when we awakened the MO from his bed he would be far from happy. He was not, having put his violin away for the night, no doubt dreaming of being a concert violinist or owning a whisky distillery! As I left the sick bay, the MO was getting his needles out to do some stitching on the Scots lad's face.

The Suez Canal – that great feat of engineering – I would drive on the road alongside the canal, it's banks littered with rusting hulks of sunken ships, having been lifted out of the canal and placed there. Situated near the middle of the canal in Bittern Lake, three captured Italian cruisers were anchored, rusting away. On the opposite side of the canal was sited a large refugee camp housing thousands of displaced people. This camp was controlled by the British Army. One of my mates, 'Rolly' Rawlins, knew a sergeant stationed at the camp. While in the area we decided to visit him. Parking our wagon, we crossed over the canal by ferry.

It was an unpleasant experience to see the conditions of extreme hardship these homeless people were living in, both old and young. Having been driven out of their own country – which country I did not know – they were now existing in a foreign land. Hundreds of small tents huddled together, lines of washing slung between them – the smoke and smells of food from field-kitchens – the stench of latrines drifting all around. The faces of these sad people told their own story. It was one of confusion and despair.

The visit turned out to be a short one, for which I was thankful. A sand-storm suddenly blew around the camp. We dashed back across the canal. The thought of having to remain overnight in the refugee camp did not appeal to me.

A few days after our visit to this camp, twenty of the refugees were brought to Shallufa to 'Star' in a documentary being filmed about refugee camps and the appalling conditions the residents were having to live under. The film makers, wishing to dramatise the film by having a sand-storm, arranged the refugees up against an aircraft parking-bay wall. Bringing an Avro Anson aircraft to the front, turned round and facing away from the refugees. With both engines running at full throttle, a very realistic sand-storm was created. The refugees were then given a good meal, bags of sweets, pop and cigarettes and driven happily back to their squalid camp.

Among the personnel at Shallufa, several of them were Jewish. One evening I had the 'honour' of taking them to RAF Tele Ka Bir to celebrate their Pesach (Passover) Festival. I was not very thrilled with the Jewish entertainment provided, nor for the Jewish food supplied, but having been given a skullcap to wear, I joined in the enthusiasm of all there and enjoyed the experience.

Having their own entertainment party, we transported them around the RAF Canal Zone camps to appear at their concerts. Returning late one night from such a show I was driving the wagon carrying the entertainers, Rolly Rawlins leading the way, driving the wagon carrying the props and costumes. He allowed the comedian of the party to drive who, in giving one of his best performances, drove the wagon into a ditch. It took us over two hours to pull the vehicle out.

Martin White was an exceptional character one could not ignore or forget. We nicknamed him, for obvious reasons, 'Fartin' Martin. When he walked into the billet he sounded like a high-powered motor cycle revving up for the TT races. When Martin was on top form, it was all hands on gas masks. The smells that came out of Suez and from the Arabs dossing down outside the camp were rose perfumed, compared to Fartin Martin.

One memorable day in the history of Shallufa saw the arrival of three new drivers. There should have been nothing spectacular about such an event, but there was. These chaps were in a class of their own, having been posted from an RAF aircrew training station at Bulawayo in Rhodesia. That evening in the billet, they held everyone spellbound. Pontoon playing ceased, letter writing stopped, the more educated ones studying the anatomy of Betty Grable had to lay the pin-ups of their favourite film star down. We sat with mouths agape, open-eyed, listening enthralled to wondrous stories about the Utopian country they had just departed from. Of days spent swimming in warm seas, nights sitting under palm trees sipping cool drinks served by dark-skinned servants, who hovered at their beck and call.

When I modestly asked them what I had been asking for over three years, they replied, "Yes, there is as much BRYLCREEM to buy as you require." That was the first and only time during my service I had contemplated deserting the RAF. Possibly, I could hitch-hike to this land of dreams.

Wearing immaculate uniforms, their hairstyles would have graced a society magazine or a Hollywood movie. We sympathised with these poor, unfortunate men having been posted to what must be the scruffiest MT section in the RAF. By the end of the evening, having had our fill of their stories, they had been nicknamed – Puff 1, Puff 2, Puff 3.

The following night the three Puffs started on about Bulawayo again. We could not stand the agony, the pontoon school had been disrupted, letters were not being written home and most important of all, studies of the anatomy of Betty Grable were being neglected. Lofty Evans came to me saying, "I'll sort these bloody puffs out, Hamby." In a loud voice, Lofty complained he could never reverse a Queen Mary (a 60 ft. articulated vehicle) into the MT repair bay in the dark. One of the Puffs (No. 2) took the bait, hook, line and sinker, saying, "No problem, I could do it easily." As we all trooped to the MT area Lofty pulled me on to one side telling me to warn the three Puffs to be on their guard, as it was a common occurrence for Arabs to slip into the camp at night and we were prone to be attacked.

Puff 2 got confidently into the cab of the Queen Mary, started the engine and attempted to reverse the wagon into the repair bay. With his two mates, Puff 1 and Puff 3 guiding him one way and ten of us advising him to take another direction, the poor devil got the articulated section of the wagon wrapped around an upright girder supporting the roof of the repair bay.

It was then noticeable, at least to us, that Lofty had disappeared. Spotting a white-sheeted figure, head covered with a red fez, I shouted, "ARABS!" We flew back to the billet leaving the Puffs, who followed close on our heels. They arrived white-faced and trembling, having left the Queen Mary still wrapped around the upright girder. A whistling Lofty later strolled into the hut without a care in the world.

Egypt, the land of the Pharaohs, is fantasised as the land of mystery and romance. I would stand outside the billet in the twilight of an evening, look towards the distant mountains at a setting sun. Behind me, a crescent moon would be rising, as twinkling stars emerged in a darkening blue sky. A camel caravan could be seen plodding slowly on it's journey across the vast desert. I would recall the musical operetta, 'The Desert Song' and it's hero, the Red Shadow, riding along with his roving band of Riffs, I would hum the music and sigh! Then from the direction of Suez, wafting in by a cooling breeze came the foul smell only Suez could give out. The romantics could keep their dreams of the mystic Middle East.

We had no idea what was happening back home. A British Forces radio station broadcast programmes from Cairo, but not possessing a wireless set in the hut, we knew little. Letters were being received from parents and girl friends. Although the war appeared to be almost over, we realised the people had their hardships with food and clothes rationing and fuel problems. Their letters never mentioned those hardships, they were always written cheerfully and with humour.

Although the main function at Shallufa was flying, there were other duties. One important task was the controlling of mosquitoes to prevent malaria. This was carried out by a gang of Arab labourers who lived in a village close to the Sweetwater Canal. Their task was to keep sections of the canal clear of weeds and fungus to prevent mosquitoes from breeding. Supervised by a corporal from Shallufa, his first job was to round the Arabs up, his second job to get them working, a thankless job. This duty was carried out once a week, for four hours during the morning before the temperature became too hot.

On one particular morning the corporal had been transported to the village by Rolly Rawlins, I had gone to Suez. On the return journey I decided to call and see Rolly. When I arrived both he and the corporal were standing in front of the wagon, Rolly wielding a starting handle, the corporal, having somehow obtained a hand scythe from one of the Arabs, was brandishing it. The Arabs were excitedly shouting and flinging their arms about as if preparing to attack Rolly and the corporal.

I sat in my cab smiling at the antics of Rolly and the corporal, then realising it could be a serious situation, I grabbed my starting handle and went and stood with them. We were surrounded by a gang of menacingly looking Arabs threatening us – 'We Three' threatening them.

All activity in the village had ceased. The elders, women and children joining their men-folk, were also circling round us – the camels had stirred from their slumbers – the oxen had stopped their monotonous trudging round the well to have a view. The Arabs must have thought I was a one-man reinforcement brigade sent to squash their rebellion.

It appeared that the Arabs were disgruntled about the rates of pay they were receiving and threatening to go on strike. After we had eventually calmed them down and peace and quiet returned, we were invited by the villagers to have coffee. We dare not refuse, otherwise it would have meant the starting handles coming out again.

Lofty Evans was the practical joker of the section, there were very few of the chaps, friend or foe, that he had not caught out. I was one of those few and proud of it, until one evening he caught me. Walking across the camp to the NAAFI with him, Lofty said, "They've got some BRYLCREEM in, Hamby." My face lit up, my heart missed an excited beat and my pace quickened to a run, Lofty running on behind. Entering the canteen and up to the counter, gasping for breath, I asked for a jar of BRYLCREEM. The chap behind the counter just looked at me for about ten eternal seconds, then nodded to a crowd of MT lads who, I had not noticed, were sat round tables close to the counter. They stood up and burst into song: -

My Brylcreem lies over the ocean,
My Brylcreem lies over the sea,
My Brylcreem lies over the ocean,
Oh, bring back my Brylcreem to me.
Bring back, bring back,
Oh, bring back my Brylcreem to me, to me,
Bring back, bring back,
Oh, bring back my Brylcreem to me.

I just stood there, a red blush appearing on my face covering my Egyptian suntan, beaming, while Lofty, with his arm round my shoulder said, "I thought I would never get you, Hamby, but I have, you owe me a pint." What Lofty or I did not realise, he had only just got me in time. My service days at Shallufa were virtually over and that was the last night I was to spend with all my MT pals.

CHAPTER TEN

TYPHOID!

The following morning I was detailed to take a wagon to Cairo to collect supplies, accompanied by Jock Douglas, the trainee driver. Jock drove to the outskirts of the Egyptian capital, I took over to drive through a busy modern Cairo, before entering the narrow streets of Old Cairo. Our destination was a large Army Supply Depot built into a mountain. From this elevated position could be seen the most impressive view of the River Nile and the Pyramids.

It was early evening before we had loaded our wagon and eaten a meal, setting off on the return journey just as dusk was falling, I decided to take the wheel all the way back to camp. Having left the outskirts of Cairo and reached the open road, I suddenly felt ill, going dizzy and having double vision. I asked Jock to take over the driving and he brought the wagon safely back to camp, Jock never having previously driven in the dark. I was too ill to tell him how grateful I was, but did thank him some months later.

Staggering into the billet at one o'clock in the morning, I was surprised to see all the lights on and everyone awake. During the evening several of the lads had been taken ill and moved to the sick bay. Tommy Sampson took one look at me and went to the sick bay, returning with the ambulance.

An amusing thing followed, although I was in no mood to smile. The medical orderly and driver, Ralph Green, (a pal) walked into the billet carrying a stretcher, the medical orderly insisting that I be carried out on it. Placing me on the stretcher, I fell off. They made three attempts to get me on to the stretcher, all of which resulted in me hitting the floor and they had not even got me to the door. I remember Ralph saying, "If you don't want to be serious Hamby, then bloody well walk!" Getting up off the floor I staggered out of the billet and climbed into the ambulance.

Arriving at the sick bay, it appeared half the personnel of the camp were patients, the medical staff had laid them out on the verandas. The MO, who, having had no time to play his violin or drink whisky that night, came and examined me. I was placed in a bed in a small ward with three other chaps, after having expected to be laid out on the veranda with all the others. The way I was feeling I could not have cared less, I just wanted to lie down.

Later that morning the MO re-appeared, saying there was a sandfly fever epidemic in the camp. For five days I remained in bed, after which I felt much better, my double vision had gone and I felt steadier. The verandas were now cleared, all the men had recovered after treatment and returned to their billets.

On the sixth day the MO came into the ward and examined me. He said I was now fully recovered, as also was 'Blondie' Haigh, one of my MT mates in the next bed. He suggested we take fourteen days leave and asked us where we would like to go, we looked at him in amazement – we were also surprised to see the MO sober. Here he was offering to arrange a leave for us. Getting over our astonishment, our first thoughts were, "Where the hell can we go?" We could have suggested England and got a dafter reply! Blondie said, "Go on Hamby, you decide. Anywhere but Egypt." I said, "Bethlehem." I do not know why

NO BRYLCREEM - NO MEDALS

I chose that place, it sounded interesting – possibly I would get some BRYLCREEM there! When the MO left with a rare sober smile on his face saying that he would arrange it, we had our first laugh for days.

The following morning, Blondie and I were placed in an ambulance and with no word of explanation taken to the 13th Army General Hospital, near Suez – the place where I had driven round the roundabout the wrong way on my second day at Shallufa. Taken into a ward, we were met by a nursing sister and told to find a bed, strip and get into it. We sat on the edge of a bed staring at each other. Blondie turned to me saying, "If this is your idea of bloody Bethlehem, Hamby, then I don't reckon much to it." After ten minutes the nursing sister returned, asking, "Why aren't you two in bed?" We replied, "We feel well!" She ordered, "Don't argue with me, do as I say and get into your beds." We did, and lay in those beds for four months. During that day a further 28 men arrived, all walking in. Six of them were not to come out alive.

The ward was to become a room of death and suffering, but on that first day we had no idea why we were there. It was to be two days later before we were told.

I was in a corner bed, the first one in the ward, Blondie in the next bed. We were the only two from the MT section. The first few days passed quickly, undergoing many tests, with strict orders from the nursing sister, who had introduced herself as Sister Bollington, not to get out of bed. Our pay books were taken from us to check if we had received all our inoculations. After two days a doctor informed us we were suffering from typhoid fever. There was an epidemic on the camp. One hundred and twenty men had caught it, sixty had been brought into this hospital and placed in two wards, sixty taken to another

Army hospital. We were warned not to write about the epidemic in our letters home, as all letters would be censored.

Blondie Haigh and I were pals, the other twenty-eight we did not know before arriving in the ward, Shallufa was a big camp. We all became close friends, apart from an SP sergeant and the Catering Officer – the one I had trouble with going out to the bomb dumps – who were also in the ward. In the bed opposite was another fair-haired youngster 'Blondie' Sutton, we immediately struck up a friendship. When Sister Bollington went off duty and with the other members of the staff not being so strict, Blondie would walk across to my bed and we played draughts.

After six days I became ill again and within three days I had lapsed into a coma, which I later understood lasted for three days. Regaining consciousness I saw the blurred vision of a figure standing by my bed. As my eyes became more adjusted I saw it was Sister Bollington, who said, "Fancy falling asleep and the War has ended, at least in Europe, but the Japanese won't last long."

It was to be a long and somewhat painful return to good health, Blondie Haigh was in a similar condition. Several of the other lads in the ward were not so lucky. One chap, a Turkish Cypriot, Abdoul, we had nick-named him 'Ali', remained in a coma for ten weeks. His wife, living in Suez, was allowed to visit him daily. Sitting by Ali's bed, her gaze never left the unconscious figure lying there. The doctor said, "He was lucky, he's sleeping through the fever." We respected his opinion.

All the men in the ward were corporals or below in rank, apart from the Catering Officer and the SP sergeant and both these had no sympathy from me. They were not happy at being placed among the lower ranks. In this unfortunate situation there was no such thing as distinction in rank. Although the officer suffered, he survived, the sergeant did not.

While lying in bed I noticed Blondie never took his eyes off the sergeant, who was suffering in agony. I said nothing, then the sergeant died. Blondie turned to me saying, "You know Hamby, when I was stationed at Dishforth in North Yorkshire that sergeant put me on a charge. Many times I wished him in hell and swore that if I ever met him in Civvy Street I would do him harm and he knew it. The first day I came through the main gate at Shallufa he was there and he remembered me, but I never thought I would see him suffer and die such an agonising death."

The poignant sounds of the suffering and the death rattles of the dying filled the ward during the heat of the day and throughout the cooler hours of the night. I lay in bed helplessly watching friends with whom I had previously talked, laughed and joked, now writhing in agony.

The doctors and nursing staff could never be praised too highly, they fought to prevent the deaths. They gave boundless time, energy and patience to alleviate the suffering. Except for the ten men who died, the staff won their battle by saving so many others from the brink of death.

THEY CAN NEVER BE FORGOTTEN BY THOSE OF US WHO SURVIVED.

When a death occurred a wagon would be sent from Shallufa to collect the body from the hospital mortuary and take it for burial. One day Tommy Sampson was detailed to come to hospital and collect my body. Before going to the mortuary he decided to visit Blondie. Looking round the door, he saw me lying in bed and almost passed out. If I had the strength, I would have got out of bed and put Tommy into it. He had been given my name instead of a chap who had died in the first bed in the next ward. Worried that my parents would be receiving notification of my death, I was assured by Sister Bollington the error had been corrected before they could be informed.

Following a death, the bed would be stripped down to the mattress and laid bare for all to see and remember it's occupant. Blondie and I were lucky in respect to having visitors. If any of our pals from Shallufa were driving in the vicinity of the hospital, they had permission from Sister Bollington to call and see us, and they came. While I was still very ill, Jock Douglas visited me. Having passed his driving test, he had driven out on his first solo journey and called to thank me for the assistance I had given him during his training. It was during this visit I was able to thank Jock for bringing me back safely from Cairo to Shallufa the night I was taken ill.

A number of us were making a gradual recovery, others more slowly, the suffering beginning to ease, there had been nine deaths in the hospital, five in our ward. We prayed and hoped there would be no more. The Cypriot, Ali, was still in a coma after six weeks, his wife making her daily vigil. She spoke little English and we could only gaze at her in admiration, the hospital staff taking care of her.

One of the lads, 'Dusty' Miller, was becoming dull-witted and restless, shouting out day and night. During the day we shouted back to him. At night, when we tried to sleep, Dusty would shout to himself.

During the early part of the morning, after breakfast had been eaten and the inside of the ward still cool, bath-time became a daily ritual. While we still lay in our beds, nurses would appear with bowls of hot water and wash our bodies. Afterwards they would re-make the beds with clean sheets. This was the most refreshing part of the day, but by mid-morning, the temperature had risen, the heat causing our newly washed bodies to sweat heavily and the clean bed-linen becoming saturated and crumpled.

Swarms of flies, which had hibernated during the night, became a daily menace. Blondie would fall asleep. As flies crawled in and out of his wide open mouth I would lean over towards his bed and with a folded magazine try to knock them away, most of the time missing the flies and hitting his face. Blondie would wake cursing and swearing as I lay innocently looking at the ceiling.

While the meals were edible, the menu never varied. During our recovery all food had to be minced. Minced chicken and porridge for breakfast, minced chicken and rice pudding for lunch and minced chicken and semolina pudding for tea. We were told we were being fed this type of food to make a lining in our stomachs, which needed strengthening.

A very pleasant and welcome addition to our diet was a daily allocation of a bottle of Jubilee Milk Stout. Looking at the label on the bottles gave me a feeling of homesickness: -

BREWED AND BOTTLED AT HOPE AND ANCHOR BREWERIES,
CLAYWHEELS LANE, SHEFFIELD, ENGLAND.

At the side of my bed a small window was built into the wall. On it's ledge were a number of old tattered books. Scrambling among them was a small lizard, I christened him

Charlie. I spent hours laid in bed watching this little chap who, during the day performed his acrobatics. At night Charlie vanished, where to I do not know. The following morning Charlie would return to give another performance. Of the books gathering dust, I read only one, Charles Dickens' 'The Old Curiosity Shop.'

As our improvement continued, Blondie Sutton resumed his visits across the ward in the evening and we played draughts. When the duty nurse was due on her rounds Blondie scampered back to his bed. One evening after having received our supper, it was lights out and we slept. Awakening next morning I looked across the ward and Blondie Sutton's bed was empty and stripped bare. It was a most bizarre experience. No one had woken during the night, no one had heard anything, yet the medical staff had attended to Blondie. He had died and been taken away. I was the last to have spoken to him. The whole ward was numbed into silence. After all we had endured, we were shocked. When Sister Bollington came on duty, I asked her what had happened and she quietly replied, "Blondie died at four o'clock this morning." Blondie seemed to have suffered less than anyone in the ward, yet he had died.

When in a position such as this, one has an abundance of time to think. I experienced what appeared to be a 'vision'. It is nothing extraordinary, just imagination, by making your mind blank to everything going on around you and concentrating on your thoughts. I was feeling extremely depressed, my thoughts centred on my parents. I knew they would be worrying about me, not knowing what my illness was.

The sound of music from a wireless in the nurses' office was drifting through to the ward. The song being played, 'I'll be seeing you.' I saw both my mother and father clearly, sitting

NO BRYLCREEM - NO MEDALS

at their small kitchen table, having a meal together as they always did. I felt I could have reached out and touched them.

The Cypriot, Ali, was still in a coma, Dusty Miller still flinging his arms about, shouting and arguing. During one of his morning rounds the doctor stood at the foot of Dusty's bed looking at him and shaking his head. One of the lads, Dave Beckett, well on his way to recovery, requested he speak to the doctor. Dave told him he could cure Dusty of his ranting and ravings. The doctor said he would be more than grateful if he could. Dave pointed out that with the men on either side of Dusty having died and both beds being empty and stripped bare, Dusty was isolated. He asked permission to be moved into one of the empty beds. The doctor advised him against it, fearing that Dusty could be violent, Dave insisted, was given permission and moved into one of the empty beds. Another of the lads 'Zeke' Shore, moved into the other empty bed. Although Dusty led them both a dog's life, with pillow fights and verbal slanging matches, they gave him back more than they received. Dave and Zeke also talked to him incessantly. They brought Dusty back to normality. I had never believed in medals, but those two lads deserved some recognition for what they did towards Dusty's recovery. Their satisfaction was the gratitude given to them by the doctor.

I had somehow lost most of my hair. I thought, "Christ, 21 years of age and bald." I had not had much time over the last three months to think about BRYLCREEM. I now thought that without my hair, I would not need any. The Good Lord up there must have heard me, it started to grow again.

The doctor, a well-respected Scotsman, together with his staff, continued to work hard and give each patient their individual attention. Another doctor was head of the hospital's department for testing blood and other samples we had to provide regularly. Having such a position, he was given the nick-name of Dracula. He was rather proud of the name and we expected him to grow fangs.

One morning I saw a large and hairy monster crawling along the bed sheets towards me, it was a Tarantula spider whose venomous bite could prove fatal. I yelled, jumped out of bed almost having a relapse. It would have been unfortunate if after all the care and attention I had received, it was a spider that got me in the end!

All through our long illness, we were only visited once by the Shallufa's Church of England padre. During his visit we were almost ignored by him, he spent most of the time speaking

Zeke Shore.

NO BRYLCREEM - NO MEDALS

to the catering officer. A Methodist padre came regularly, speaking to every man individually. He also wrote to the next of kin of those who had died, irrespective of their religion. On one of his visits this padre asked me where my home town was, then told me that he had preached at a Methodist church opposite Hillsborough Park, in Sheffield.

We had only one visit by Shallufa's MO, the reason later became obvious. When the illnesses were confirmed as typhoid fever and considered to be of epidemic proportions, an investigation team was brought into Shallufa to trace it's source. They carried out a routine check, testing water supplies and finding it clear, the team then requested a list of all the personnel who had contracted the disease. It was observed that of the 120 men having typhoid, only two were above the rank of corporal, the catering officer and the sergeant policeman. It was then discovered that when he was duty officer, the catering officer ate in the other ranks dining hall. The sergeant policeman, also when on duty had food sent to him from the other ranks kitchen.

Suspicion fell on the kitchen staff. Carrying out a physical examination on all who worked in that dining hall, an Arab labourer who did menial tasks was identified as a typhoid carrier. This man should have received a strict medical examination prior to being given this work. The MO was held responsible. It was understood he was sent back to England, although I never had confirmation of that, we never saw him again.

Of the 120 men who had caught typhoid fever, 24 had died, 10 in our hospital, 6 in our ward, 4 in the next ward and 14 in the other hospital. Both hospitals and doctors had treated their patients by a different method, we appeared to have been

'Guinea Pigs.' Our doctor and his staff were delighted that there had been fewer fatalities under their care.

After four months, we were finally on the road to recovery and although still weak, we were able to get out of bed. Ali', having regained consciousness, but still in bed, his wife's vigil had been rewarded. Dusty Miller was back to normal and wondering what all the fuss over him had been about. Dave Beckett and Zeke Shore, having cured him, were both on the verge of a nervous breakdown. When we warned them that they would be placed in the capable hands of Dusty, they were instantly cured.

Sister Bollington, attractive, stern, but very fair, possessed a wonderful sense of humour. One of the ward nurses was, amazingly, a German. Built like a tank and as tough, she revelled in swearing at us (in German). Almost recovered, I caught Impetigo. 'Fraulein' would daub my itchy spots with lots of gentian violet, a horrible blue ointment. Turning me over roughly on to my stomach, she would paint a face on my backside where there were no spots, saying, "Un Gott, Viggle Dat."

The doctor and Sister Bollington walked into the ward one morning, over four months after we had first entered it, informing us that rather than sending us convalescing, it had been decided that the ward was to be converted into a convalescence room. After three weeks we should be fit enough to return to Shallufa. Overnight, an amazing transformation took place to the ward, small bed-side reading lamps, tables and easy chairs appeared. I have no idea where they came from.

In the heat of the day we were supplied with bottles of cold water and orange squash, but within minutes of receiving them they were warm. Our commanding officer at Shallufa arranged for champagne and eau-de-cologne to be flown in from South Africa, the champagne to cheer us up, the eau-de-cologne to cool us down.

Blondie Haigh suddenly claimed he was a Salvationist – he had never mentioned this to me before and judging by his language, he kept forgetting it – and champagne drinking was strictly forbidden. I had to swap him half of my orange squash for his champagne. I hated the damn stuff. Blondie had craftily thought of the Salvationist idea before I did. We were still being supplied daily with a bottle of Jubilee Milk Stout.

One of the most amazing happenings during my lengthy stay in hospital was that little lizard, Charlie. I have written that when I was very ill, I laid for hours looking at Charlie doing his acrobatics on the shelf amongst the old, tattered books. Now, when I had almost recovered, Charlie vanished. After all the suffering we had endured and the heartaches of losing friends during the previous four months, I shall always believe that little fellow, Charlie, appeared daily to help me through a crisis.

The doctor and the nursing staff decided to hold a party in the ward. The two doctors (Dracula's department had baked a cake, we refused to give blood for it) and Sister Bollington really let their hair down. Our commanding officer, who had, throughout our illnesses, been in constant touch with the doctors and making regular visits, (but not in his old Wellington Bomber) also came.

Entertainment was by Dave Beckett, giving his impression of motorcycle riding in the TT races, he nearly won, but fell off the form at the last bend. Fraulein, the German nurse gave her own inimitable impersonation of Marlene Dietrich singing 'Lilli Marlene', while Zeke Shore, equally as mad and Dusty Miller (who by his antics had us doubting his recovery) performed brilliantly as Flanagan and Allen. The party, which had been a huge success, ended with a talcum powder fight.

When all was over and the ward became quiet, one could feel the sombre thoughts of everyone for those missing mates. The six empty beds, stripped of their coverings were still there to remember their late occupants.

Two days later the doctor informed us we would not be returning to Shallufa, we were to be invalided home. In the afternoon we descended on the market place of Suez for souvenirs and presents for our families, the doctors, Sister Bollington and the nurses.

The following day a vehicle came from Shallufa to take us to collect our kit and say goodbye to our mates. Driving it was Jock Douglas. All our mates were there, Rommel, (without his greatcoat touching his toes) Drummy Drummond, Rolly

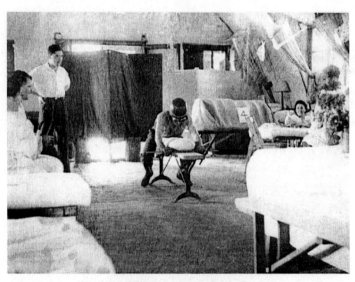

Hospital 'TT Races' with Dave Beckett.

NO BRYLCREEM - NO MEDALS

Rawlins, Tommy Sampson and Lofty Evans, telling me, "They've got some BRYLCREEM in the NAAFI, Hamby." Fartin Martin was there to put on a special farewell show. The 3 Puff's were absent, still trying to untangle the Queen Mary they had wrapped around the MT bay girder, over 4 months previously.

The lads were on stand-by for Burma, I had missed that, possibly I may have got some BRYLCREEM there. When Jock drove out of the camp gates on our return to the hospital I looked back, remembering the day, 15 months previously, when I had entered them for the first time (slightly inebriated), never imagining the tragedies I would be involved in and the suffering I would see and experience.

The Author and Tommy Sampson.

CHAPTER ELEVEN

GOODBYE TO ALL THAT

Within two days we were on our way, departing on a train from Suez to Port Said. I prayed that providing the troopship taking me home did not stray off course and hit an iceberg, then I would make it safely back to England.

Before boarding the troopship, I went into a forces canteen on the quayside at Port Said. An airman seated at a table shouted my name and came and embraced me, looking as if he had seen a ghost. It was Ben Stacey, one of the six merry lads from the airfield construction days in England, from whom I had been separated at Heliopolis. He said he knew I had been posted to Shallufa and had visited the camp, he called at the MT section only to be told I had died of typhoid fever. Ben must have called at the camp on the same day that Tommy Sampson had gone to hospital to collect my body and take me to my 'funeral', Ben had seen a ghost in the flesh.

We boarded the troopship, Canton, which sailed out and away from Port Said and Egypt. No anchoring and staying in the middle of a river for fourteen days, as the Tecleberg had done coming out of Port Glasgow. The Canton, a large ex-passenger liner, now classed as a semi-hospital/troopship, was carrying over two thousand men, some, like myself being invalided home, others returning for early demobilisation. We were well fed – no class distinction – looked after and informed of passing places of interest. It was almost like a cruise, but alas

NO BRYLCREEM - NO MEDALS

they did not sell BRYLCREEM, having plenty of that bloody Anzora, chocolate and Lux toilet soap. My unpleasant memories of the Tecleberg were soon forgotten.

On board the Canton, there were light-hearted moments. One of the lads possessed a copy of that not to be read naughty book, 'Lady Chatterley's Lover'. We sat round in a group eagerly reading of the capers of Lady Chatterley and her gamekeeper, then flung it in the Mediterranean for the fishes to read. When someone opened a case and a scorpion crawled out, we nearly followed the book into the sea! After we had dined one evening, a nut-case washed all the knives, forks and spoons in a large bucket, then threw the dirty water into the Bay of Biscay, forgetting to take the cutlery out! We were scrounging for replacements or eating with our fingers.

Arriving at Southampton, the Canton docked alongside the liner Queen Mary. A lone soldier, among the two thousand aboard the ship, noticed and let it be known in a loud voice, that flying from the mast of the Queen Mary (used as a troopship for the USA forces) was a flag bearing the Stars and Stripes of America. There was an immediate rush of all aboard to one side of the Canton. The ship appeared to be in danger of keeling over as boos and jeers were aimed at the Queen Mary. This completely drowned the music of the bandsmen, who having arrived running and puffing along the quayside to welcome us home, were endeavouring to play 'We'll gather lilacs.'

Disembarking from the Canton we were transported by coach (not on the back of the 3-ton Bedford lorry I had expected) to Southampton railway station, then to the RAF Hospital at Melksham, in Wiltshire, where we stayed for six days, having to undergo thorough medical examinations and take daily baths.

The night before we were to return to our homes on leave we said our farewells over beers in the NAAFI canteen. Blondie Haigh, (having forgotten he was a Salvationist) – Dave Beckett, (still ambitious to win the TT races) – Zeke Shore – Dusty Miller and others. We had left the Cypriot lad, Ali, behind with his devoted wife in Suez. Little was said about the previous five months. Of our missing mates, we kept our thoughts to ourselves.

Boarding trains to our respective homes, once again I was travelling alone. I arrived in Sheffield on a Saturday afternoon. The barrage balloons had disappeared. Sheffield was finally at peace, but with plenty of scars to show what the city and it's people had experienced.

Leaning out of the carriage window, I saw the lonely figure of my father standing on the platform eagerly watching the slowing train. It was a meeting I had once doubted would ever take place. As we walked to the nearby Gambit cafe, my father asked me about my illness. Both my mother and father had spent five months worrying about me and I had been in no position to tell them what that illness was. Later that day I was re-united with my mother, who was more concerned about my having returned weighing eight and a half stone and resembling a skeleton, than whatever had caused it.

Although I had written to a number of girls while in the Middle East, I considered myself unattached and had every intention of remaining that way. Within thirty hours of getting off the train in Sheffield I met the beautiful girl with whom I fell in love and later married. I was still in the RAF, but for how long I did not know.

NO BRYLCREEM - NO MEDALS

Before leaving hospital at RAF Melksham to return home on leave I had been given a form to fill in, requesting me to choose at which camp I would prefer to be stationed, after my leave. I wrote down three camps as near to Sheffield as possible. With my luck, as in the past, I did not hold out much hope of being posted to one. I was fortunate, I was sent to Finningley, near Doncaster. As I sauntered through the main gate a service policeman – a pity it was not Our Harry – bawled at me, "LAC, put your cap on!" I had forgotten I was no longer part of the scruffy MT at Shallufa.

In the NAAFI on the first evening, I asked the young assistant for a jar of BRYLCREEM. The lad, still wet behind the ears from the last time his mother had washed them and his spotty face sporting a fuzzy beard he was trying to grow, looked sadly at me before disappearing into a back room. Returning with the manager who, in his most officious manner demanded, "What do you want?" I replied, "A jar of BRYLCREEM." Stretching up to his full height of five foot six inches and letting me know of his important position as NAAFI manager, he said, "Don't you know there's been a bloody war on, where were you when WE were fighting it." I said, "On a Cook's Tour of Egypt." He replied, "I didn't know they did them. Anyhow, we haven't any BRYLCREEM, only bloody Anzora!"

Life at Finningley could not be compared to that which I had experienced on previous camps. The whole atmosphere lacked enthusiasm. There was no comradeship among the men. I soon became dispirited. I went into nearby Doncaster one afternoon and in a cafe met Bomber Lancaster, with whom I had been stationed on the Shetlands. Bomber, still a corporal, was on his way to an RAF station near York.

I wangled a transfer to RAF Scofton near Worksop. Scofton, a satellite-station of Finningley, was an unusual aerodrome, there were no planes or any flying. If an aeroplane actually flew over the camp the personnel considered it a big occasion and raised a flag. What it had been used for during the war I do not know. Many years later I met a person who had been a civilian employee at Scofton during the war and she told me that it had been a very busy aerodrome. I considered Scofton to be a cushy posting. I could catch a bus at the end of the lane directly to Sheffield. I would have been content to remain there for the remainder of my service, but alas that was not to be.

Called into the camp office one morning I was supplied with a travel warrant and told to report to RAF Weeton, near Blackpool. I was to take an examination for driving instructor. Not wanting to leave Scofton, I felt confident I could fix it to fail the test.

On arrival at Weeton I stayed the evening in a hut with another 10 chaps, who like myself had been stationed overseas, returned home and got cushy postings and were now faced with the prospect of being moved. We were all of the same mind, we were going to flop the driving test.

RAF Weeton had a few memories for me as I had taken my driving course there four years previously. It was the first of many NAAFI's I was to visit in my unsuccessful quests for BRYLCREEM. Surely, now the war was over, supplies of my favourite hair-cream would have returned to normal? I entered the NAAFI with great optimism. The chap behind the counter greeted me as a long-lost friend. As I asked for a jar of BRYLCREEM, he said, "I thought it was you, you came in here four years ago. I've never forgotten the welcome you received." He bent down beneath the counter. I thought,

"Success at last!" Straightening up, he smiled, "Sorrow, old chum, no BRYLCREEM, but have a free jar of bloody Anzora!"

The following morning, five of us were taken out in a 15 cwt Bedford, the easiest of vehicles to drive. Driving around Blackpool, our concentration was on the sights and not on the driving. I have never heard so many tunes played on a gearbox. It must have been a wonderful experience for the sergeant examining us. He was not to be deceived and we all passed. So began another period of sufferance. I was determined my career as a driving instructor would not last long.

When the war ended all RAF personnel who had been trained as aircrew became redundant and they were required to re-muster to various trades. Several of them selected MT driving. Our duties were to train them. Immediately a problem arose, these bods having attained aircrew ranks of between sergeant and warrant officer and still retaining those ranks believed they were more superior to we mere corporals. This we were not prepared to tolerate. Only after ratification by senior officers on our part did the training programme proceed smoothly.

Life became dangerous and perilous. Out driving on the roads, these ex-aircrew types were still of the opinion they were flying planes in the open skies. Most of the training was in convoys. This lot did not believe in foot brakes, the only way they could stop a wagon was to hit the one in front.

The end came for me one afternoon on the outskirts of Blackpool. Driving a 3-ton Bedford Wagon, the trainee driver misjudged a roundabout, mounted a pavement, going round a lamp standard on to a shopping forecourt. With the engine being in the middle of the cab, I was unable to reach over and grab the hand brake. Amazingly, there were no people outside the shops, otherwise someone would have been killed.

On our return to camp I requested an interview with the officer in charge of the MT school. I explained I had been driving for over four years without an accident or causing damage to a vehicle – not mentioning my wild drive through the forest in West Sussex – and was in danger of being killed at any time. He sympathised with me saying there was nothing he could do about it and I was to remain as an instructor. The following week the officer suffered a nervous breakdown.

I had decided enough was enough and recalled what the doctor had told me on my discharge from hospital in Egypt, "If you should feel ill, report sick immediately." I did, complaining of stomach pains, believing them to be the after effects of typhoid fever. I was then informed my medical records had been lost. I believe this was done deliberately to stop me from applying for an invalidity pension when I left the service. I was taken off instructing.

While home on a weekend leave for my engagement party, accompanied by another lad, 'Taffy' Williams, I was taken genuinely ill. The morning I was to return to Weeton I was too ill to return to camp and Taffy had to return to Weeton alone. I went to see the local doctor, who was not interested in my illness. He sent me to a nearby hospital treating wounded military personnel – the hospital was also not interested. I was then sent to a small Army military hospital on the other side of Sheffield. By this time I was feeling so ill that I thought my time to expire had finally arrived.

The hospital, Snaithing Grange Lodge, was a large house situated in the residential area of Fulwood. Before the war it had been the residence of a wealthy Sheffield industrialist.

Commandeered by the Army during the war, it could only be described as the most extraordinary and humorous hospital the Army possessed.

I was placed in a room with 15 other chaps. I appeared to be the only patient in the ward genuinely ill. The others were either malingerers or deserters. After examination by a doctor, my illness was diagnosed as Tonsillitis.

The goings on in Snaithing Grange Lodge were hilarious twenty-four hours a day. The other 'patients' were born actors. When the doctor made his rounds after breakfast they would start moaning and groaning when he reached the foot of their bed. He was no fool and appeared to be wise to their antics, playing up to them by prescribing medicine intended to make anyone ill. After the doctor had left the ward, the medical orderly remained, asking if anyone wanted horse racing bets placing. The bets were then taken in the Army ambulance to a bookmaker in Sheffield. The ATS ambulance driver, Joan Smith, a Sheffield girl, had attended the same school as me.

Snaithing Grange

A deserter was carried in one morning. While being chased by the military police over a railway track he had fallen between the lines, breaking his ankle. Along with myself, he was the only other genuine patient in the ward.

Afternoon was a restful period, with most of the patients having been out on the town until the early hours of the morning, they had to have their 'siesta'. Evening visiting times were far from peaceful, there were more girls trying to get into bed with their boy friends than there were trying to keep out. The lad in the next bed, another deserter, greeted his girl friend each night by punching her between the eyes. She never missed a visit and sported two black eyes all the time I was there.

After visiting hours were over and supper eaten, most of the patients in the ward were taken to Sheffield in the ambulance driven by Joan and left to pub crawl in the city. Returning, two by two, during the early hours of the morning, there would be a constant banging on the French windows to be let in. After 14 days, during which time I never had a wink of proper sleep, I was glad to get back to Weeton for a rest.

Back once more at Weeton, I was informed I had been posted to Burma. My mates from Shallufa who were now out there must have been asking for me. Possibly Lofty Evans had at last got me a jar of BRYLCREEM! There was no way I was going to leave that lovely girl in Sheffield, so I reported sick again. The posting was either cancelled or they sent someone else, I had no conscience about this, it was their problem.

Returning to Weeton one Monday morning after a weekend leave and while waiting at the Sheffield Midland Railway Station, I met a young lad from Stocksbridge, a new RAF recruit also returning to Weeton. We travelled together, fell asleep on the train, went past Manchester and awoke at Carlisle.

Eventually arriving back at Weeton late in the afternoon, the poor devil was scared stiff. I told him to walk through the main gate and leave it to me, I spoke to the SP there, explaining what had happened and it was all right. Shortly after, that same lad came home on leave and was killed in a road accident.

Finally came my Demob. On the 9th December 1946, I travelled the short distance down the road from RAF Weeton to RAF Kirkham. I walked into a hut and found a bed for the night. Sitting on the next bed reading a book was Taffy Austin, my old mate from Noss Hill on the Shetlands. We had to meet again. Taffy had been in Germany. We talked into the night swapping experiences. I asked him about his mother, whose many letters had meant so much to him and he sadly told me that she had passed away. We exchanged addresses and promised to keep in touch. We did so and he came to my wedding in 1948. I have not heard from him since.

The following morning, 10th December, 1946, was exactly four years and five months to the day that I had left Sheffield clutching a small brown attaché case – I never knew what happened to that case. I went in front of an officer who promised me a wonderful future if I stayed in the Royal Air Force.

I looked, I smiled, I said "No Thanks!"

Only the promise of a posting to Bulawayo in Rhodesia, with lazy days by the sea, servants to wait on me hand and foot under the swaying Palm trees and an unlimited supply of BRYLCREEM would have made me consider staying in the Royal Air Force.

I received my Demob suit and judging by the way it fitted, it must have been issued by that same sergeant who had given me my first uniform at Cardington.

Transported by an ever-faithful 3-ton Bedford wagon to Preston railway station, I boarded a train and after travelling all alone again, arrived in Sheffield. I was a CIVVY!

During the whole of my service days, of all the places I went to, I never did get any Brylcreem, and the RAF never gave me a service medal, just a tattered old pay book!

The Author and pal in an RAF Crash Tender.

NO BRYLCREEM - NO MEDALS